Walt Disney's Donald Duck in CLAUS and EFFECT

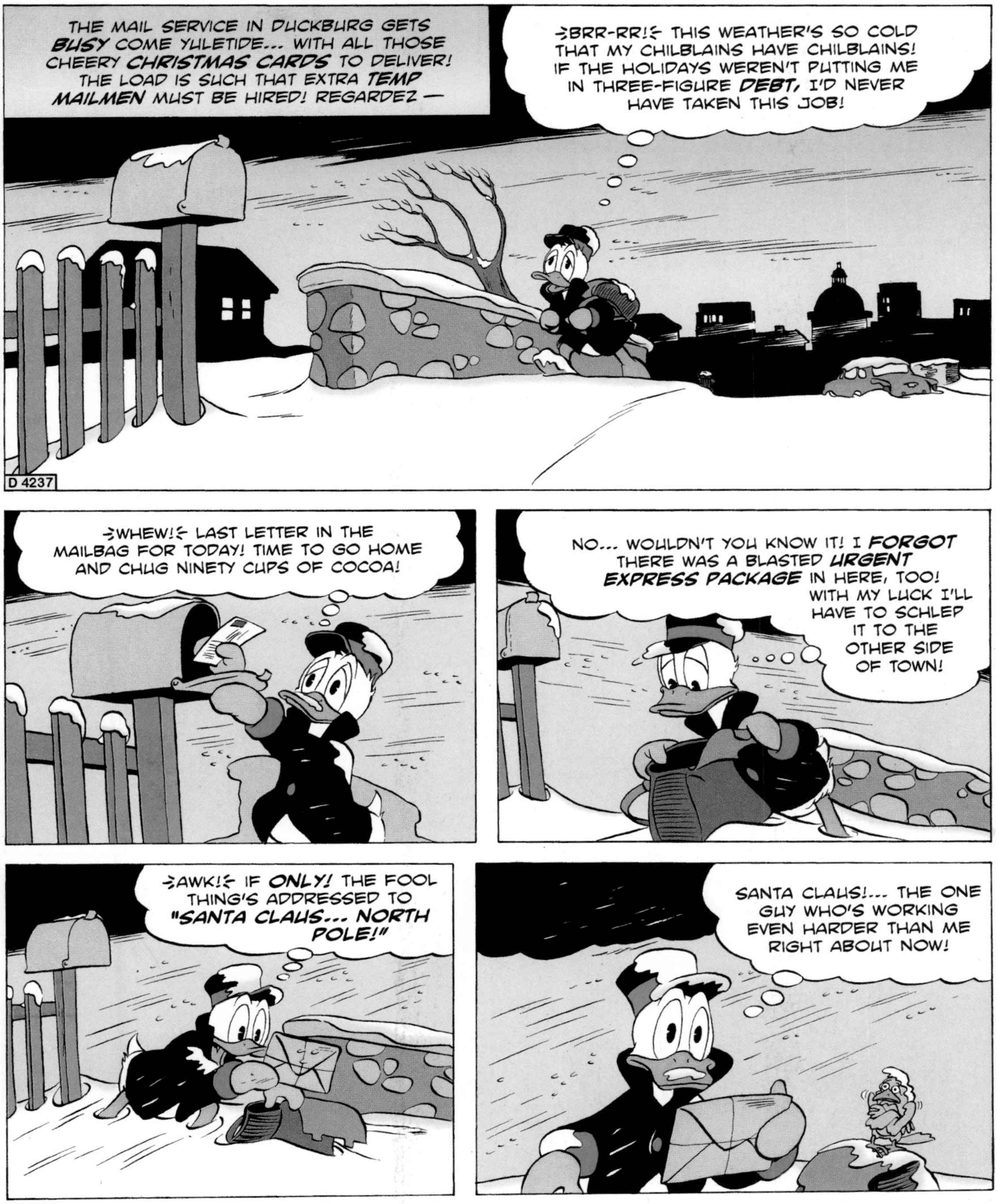
THE MAIL SERVICE IN DUCKBURG GETS BUSY COME YULETIDE... WITH ALL THOSE CHEERY CHRISTMAS CARDS TO DELIVER! THE LOAD IS SUCH THAT EXTRA TEMP MAILMEN MUST BE HIRED! REGARDEZ —
BRR-RR! THIS WEATHER'S SO COLD THAT MY CHILBLAINS HAVE CHILBLAINS! IF THE HOLIDAYS WEREN'T PUTTING ME IN THREE-FIGURE DEBT, I'D NEVER HAVE TAKEN THIS JOB!
D 4237
WHEW! LAST LETTER IN THE MAILBAG FOR TODAY! TIME TO GO HOME AND CHUG NINETY CUPS OF COCOA!
NO... WOULDN'T YOU KNOW IT! I FORGOT THERE WAS A BLASTED URGENT EXPRESS PACKAGE IN HERE, TOO! WITH MY LUCK I'LL HAVE TO SCHLEP IT TO THE OTHER SIDE OF TOWN!
AWK! IF ONLY! THE FOOL THING'S ADDRESSED TO "SANTA CLAUS... NORTH POLE!"
SANTA CLAUS!... THE ONE GUY WHO'S WORKING EVEN HARDER THAN ME RIGHT ABOUT NOW!

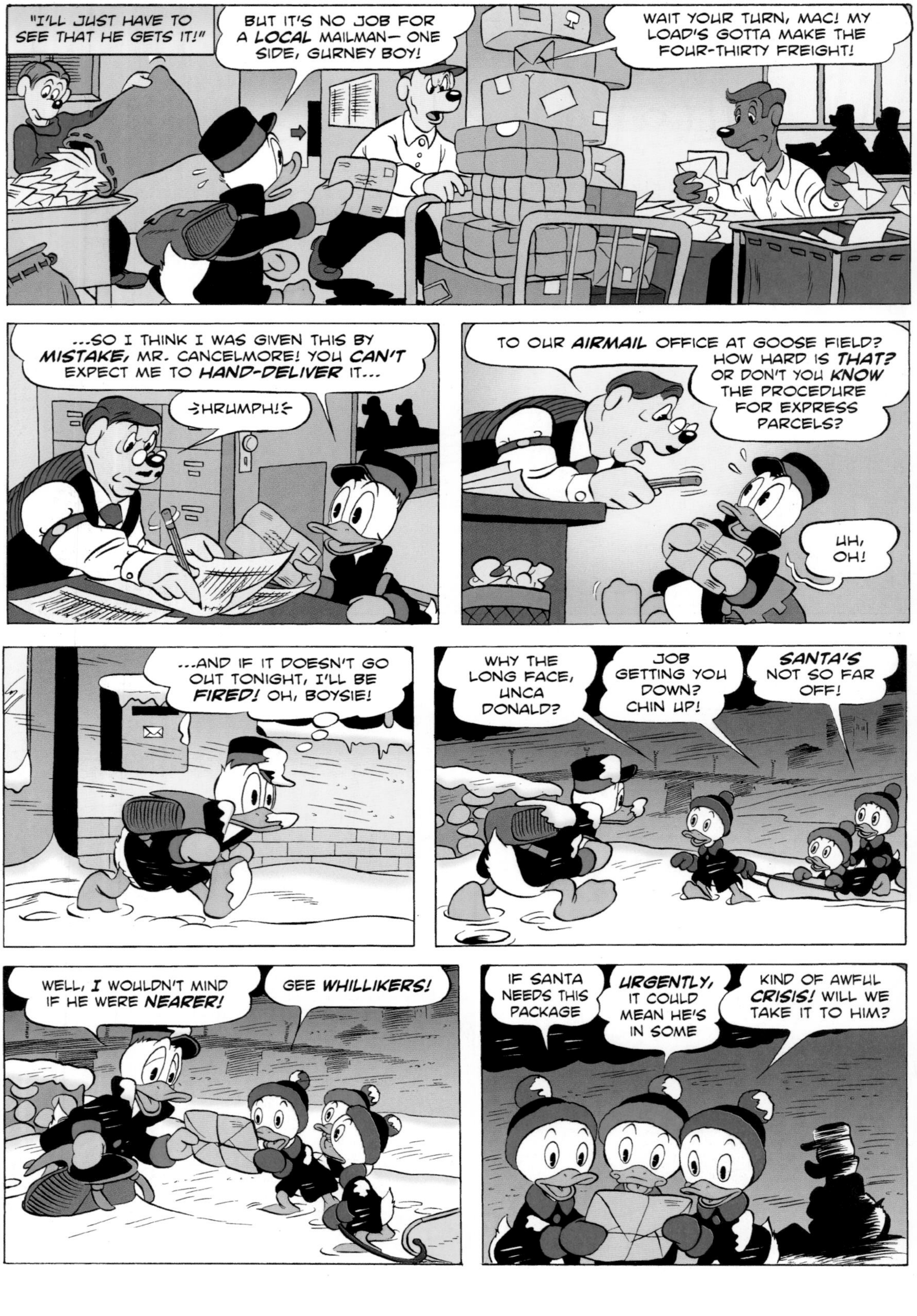
"I'LL JUST HAVE TO SEE THAT HE GETS IT!"
BUT IT'S NO JOB FOR A LOCAL MAILMAN— ONE SIDE, GURNEY BOY!
WAIT YOUR TURN, MAC! MY LOAD'S GOTTA MAKE THE FOUR-THIRTY FREIGHT!
...SO I THINK I WAS GIVEN THIS BY MISTAKE, MR. CANCELMORE! YOU CAN'T EXPECT ME TO HAND-DELIVER IT...
HRUMPH!
TO OUR AIRMAIL OFFICE AT GOOSE FIELD? HOW HARD IS THAT? OR DON'T YOU KNOW THE PROCEDURE FOR EXPRESS PARCELS?
UH, OH!
...AND IF IT DOESN'T GO OUT TONIGHT, I'LL BE FIRED! OH, BOYSIE!
WHY THE LONG FACE, UNCA DONALD?
JOB GETTING YOU DOWN? CHIN UP!
SANTA'S NOT SO FAR OFF!
WELL, I WOULDN'T MIND IF HE WERE NEARER!
GEE WHILLIKERS!
IF SANTA NEEDS THIS PACKAGE
URGENTLY, IT COULD MEAN HE'S IN SOME
KIND OF AWFUL CRISIS! WILL WE TAKE IT TO HIM?

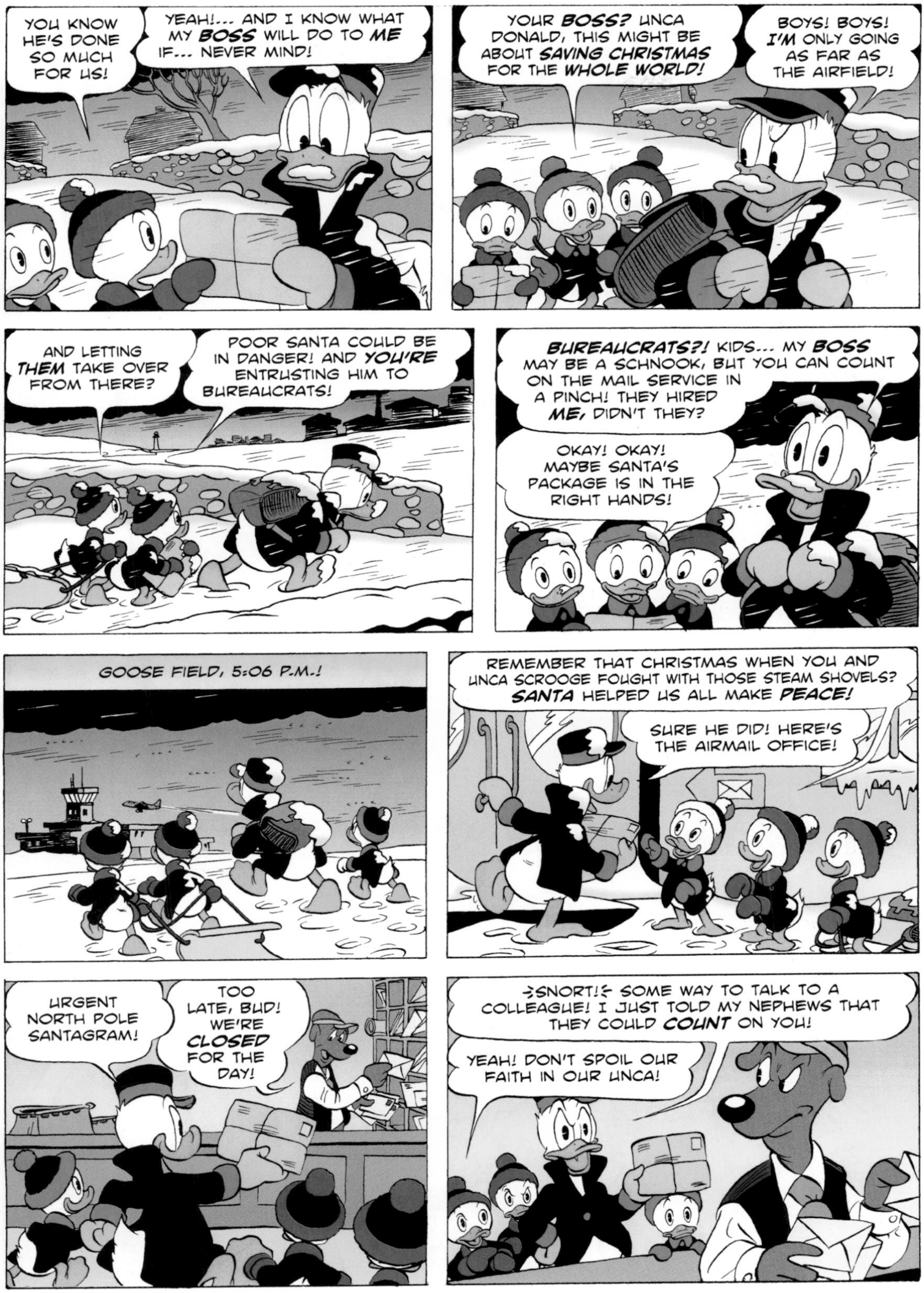
YOU KNOW HE'S DONE SO MUCH FOR US!
YEAH!... AND I KNOW WHAT MY BOSS WILL DO TO ME IF... NEVER MIND!
YOUR BOSS? UNCA DONALD, THIS MIGHT BE ABOUT SAVING CHRISTMAS FOR THE WHOLE WORLD!
BOYS! BOYS! I'M ONLY GOING AS FAR AS THE AIRFIELD!
AND LETTING THEM TAKE OVER FROM THERE?
POOR SANTA COULD BE IN DANGER! AND YOU'RE ENTRUSTING HIM TO BUREAUCRATS!
BUREAUCRATS?! KIDS... MY BOSS MAY BE A SCHNOOK, BUT YOU CAN COUNT ON THE MAIL SERVICE IN A PINCH! THEY HIRED ME, DIDN'T THEY?
OKAY! OKAY! MAYBE SANTA'S PACKAGE IS IN THE RIGHT HANDS!
GOOSE FIELD, 5:06 P.M.!
REMEMBER THAT CHRISTMAS WHEN YOU AND UNCA SCROOGE FOUGHT WITH THOSE STEAM SHOVELS? SANTA HELPED US ALL MAKE PEACE!
SURE HE DID! HERE'S THE AIRMAIL OFFICE!
URGENT NORTH POLE SANTAGRAM!
TOO LATE, BUD! WE'RE CLOSED FOR THE DAY!
SNORT! SOME WAY TO TALK TO A COLLEAGUE! I JUST TOLD MY NEPHEWS THAT THEY COULD COUNT ON YOU!
YEAH! DON'T SPOIL OUR FAITH IN OUR UNCA!

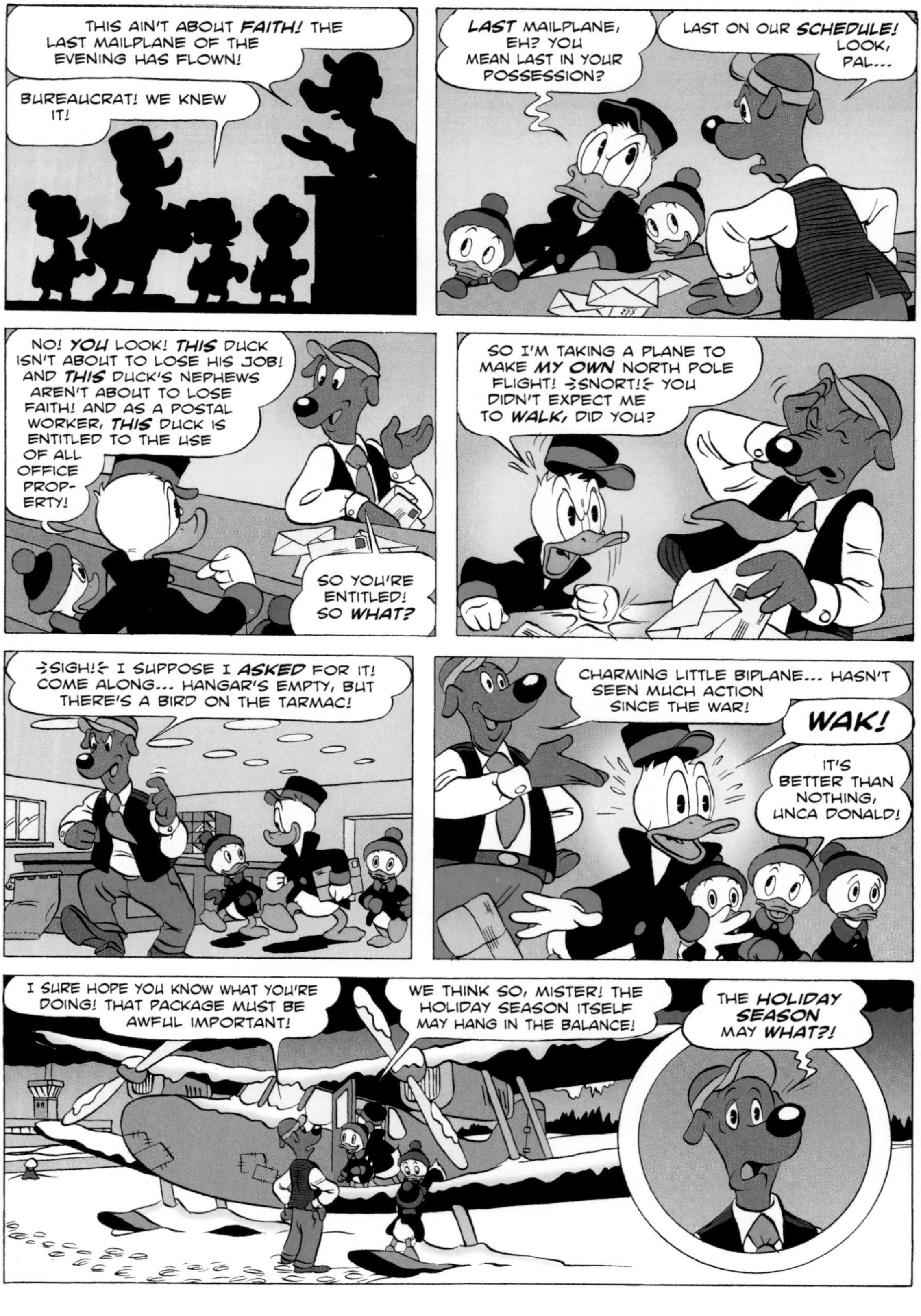
THIS AIN'T ABOUT FAITH! THE LAST MAILPLANE OF THE EVENING HAS FLOWN!
BUREAUCRAT! WE KNEW IT!
LAST MAILPLANE, EH? YOU MEAN LAST IN YOUR POSSESSION?
LAST ON OUR SCHEDULE! LOOK, PAL...
NO! YOU LOOK! THIS DUCK ISN'T ABOUT TO LOSE HIS JOB! AND THIS DUCK'S NEPHEWS AREN'T ABOUT TO LOSE FAITH! AND AS A POSTAL WORKER, THIS DUCK IS ENTITLED TO THE USE OF ALL OFFICE PROPERTY!
SO YOU'RE ENTITLED! SO WHAT?
SO I'M TAKING A PLANE TO MAKE MY OWN NORTH POLE FLIGHT! ⇒SNORT!⇐ YOU DIDN'T EXPECT ME TO WALK, DID YOU?
⇒SIGH!⇐ I SUPPOSE I ASKED FOR IT! COME ALONG... HANGAR'S EMPTY, BUT THERE'S A BIRD ON THE TARMAC!
CHARMING LITTLE BIPLANE... HASN'T SEEN MUCH ACTION SINCE THE WAR!
WAK!
IT'S BETTER THAN NOTHING, UNCA DONALD!
I SURE HOPE YOU KNOW WHAT YOU'RE DOING! THAT PACKAGE MUST BE AWFUL IMPORTANT!
WE THINK SO, MISTER! THE HOLIDAY SEASON ITSELF MAY HANG IN THE BALANCE!
THE HOLIDAY SEASON MAY WHAT?!

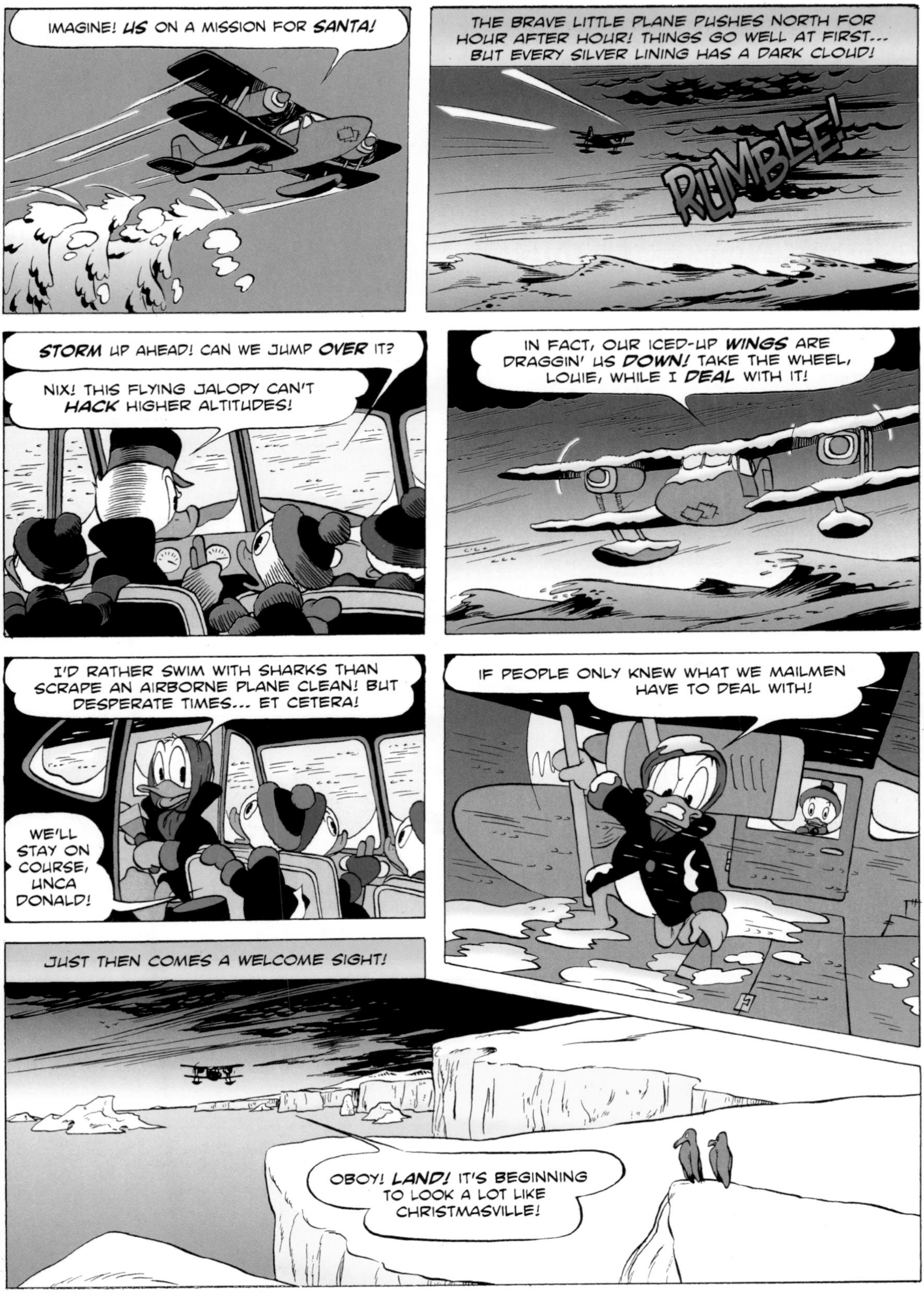
IMAGINE! US ON A MISSION FOR SANTA!
THE BRAVE LITTLE PLANE PUSHES NORTH FOR HOUR AFTER HOUR! THINGS GO WELL AT FIRST... BUT EVERY SILVER LINING HAS A DARK CLOUD!
RUMBLE!
STORM UP AHEAD! CAN WE JUMP OVER IT?
NIX! THIS FLYING JALOPY CAN'T HACK HIGHER ALTITUDES!
IN FACT, OUR ICED-UP WINGS ARE DRAGGIN' US DOWN! TAKE THE WHEEL, LOUIE, WHILE I DEAL WITH IT!
I'D RATHER SWIM WITH SHARKS THAN SCRAPE AN AIRBORNE PLANE CLEAN! BUT DESPERATE TIMES... ET CETERA!
WE'LL STAY ON COURSE, UNCA DONALD!
IF PEOPLE ONLY KNEW WHAT WE MAILMEN HAVE TO DEAL WITH!
JUST THEN COMES A WELCOME SIGHT!
OBOY! LAND! IT'S BEGINNING TO LOOK A LOT LIKE CHRISTMASVILLE!

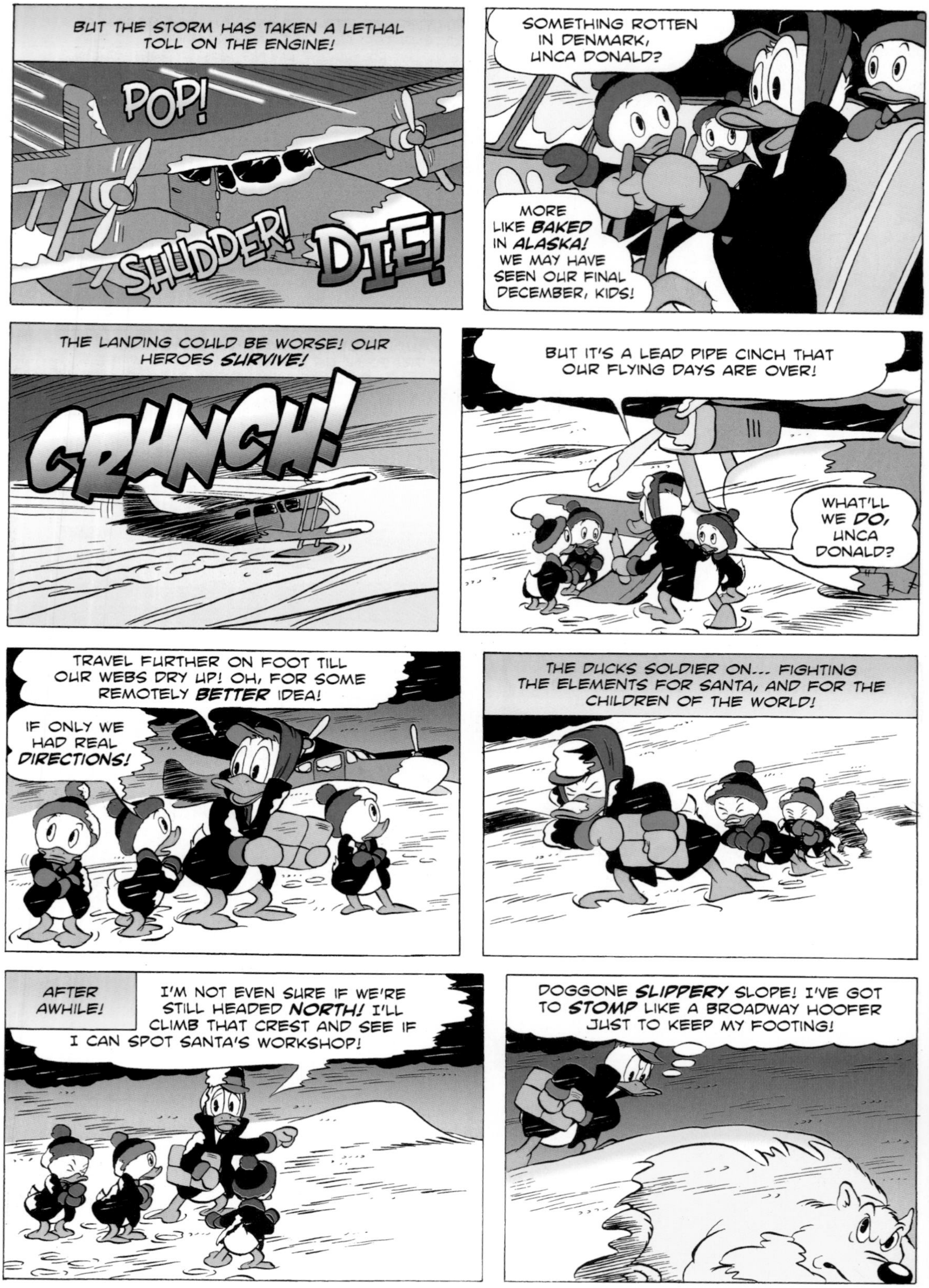
BUT THE STORM HAS TAKEN A LETHAL TOLL ON THE ENGINE!
POP!
SHUDDER!
DIE!
SOMETHING ROTTEN IN DENMARK, UNCA DONALD?
MORE LIKE BAKED IN ALASKA! WE MAY HAVE SEEN OUR FINAL DECEMBER, KIDS!
THE LANDING COULD BE WORSE! OUR HEROES SURVIVE!
CRUNCH!
BUT IT'S A LEAD PIPE CINCH THAT OUR FLYING DAYS ARE OVER!
WHAT'LL WE DO, UNCA DONALD?
TRAVEL FURTHER ON FOOT TILL OUR WEBS DRY UP! OH, FOR SOME REMOTELY BETTER IDEA!
IF ONLY WE HAD REAL DIRECTIONS!
THE DUCKS SOLDIER ON... FIGHTING THE ELEMENTS FOR SANTA, AND FOR THE CHILDREN OF THE WORLD!
AFTER AWHILE!
I'M NOT EVEN SURE IF WE'RE STILL HEADED NORTH! I'LL CLIMB THAT CREST AND SEE IF I CAN SPOT SANTA'S WORKSHOP!
DOGGONE SLIPPERY SLOPE! I'VE GOT TO STOMP LIKE A BROADWAY HOOFER JUST TO KEEP MY FOOTING!

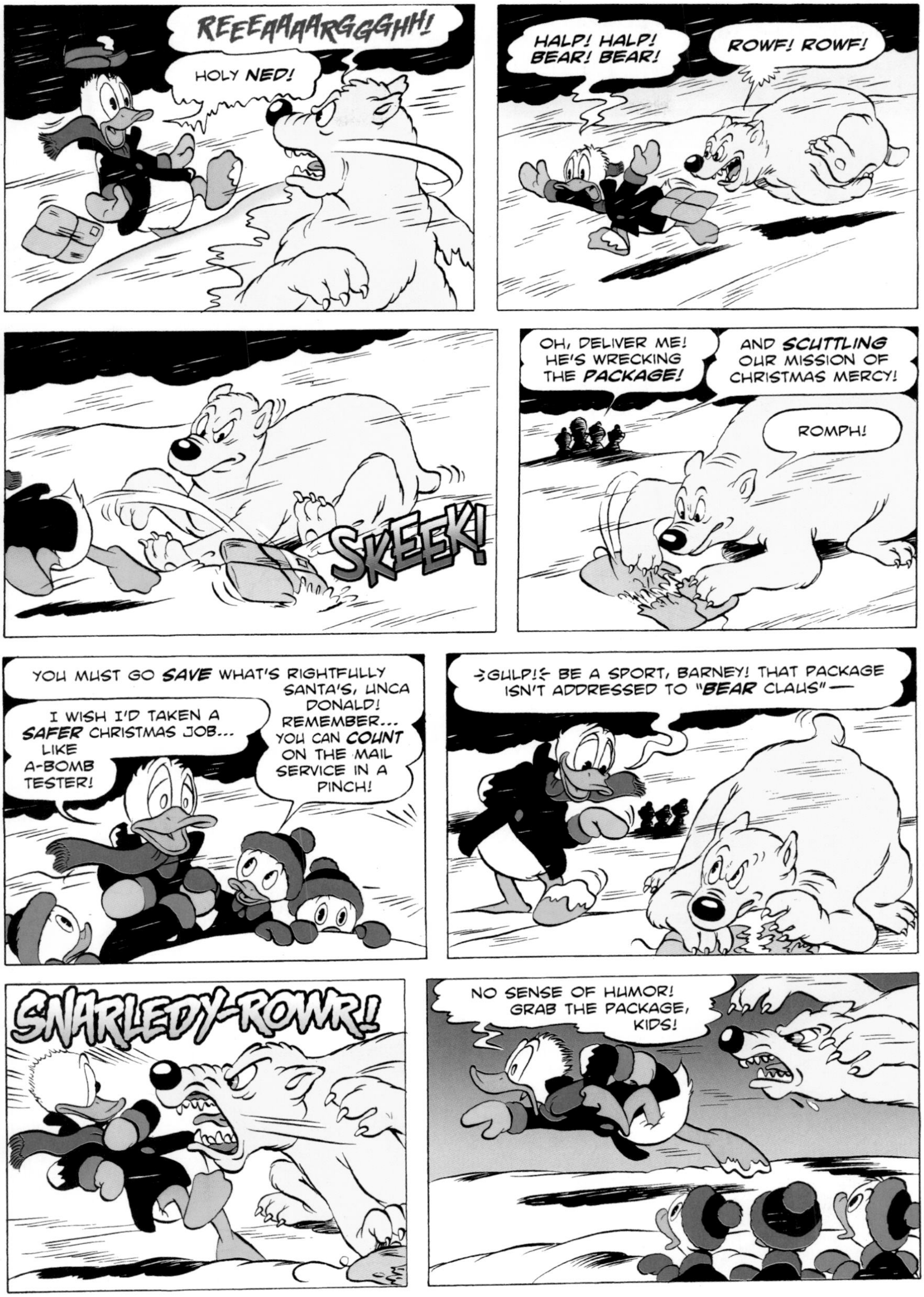
REEEAAAARGGGHH!
HOLY NED!
HALP! HALP! BEAR! BEAR!
ROWF! ROWF!
SKEEK!
OH, DELIVER ME! HE'S WRECKING THE PACKAGE!
AND SCUTTLING OUR MISSION OF CHRISTMAS MERCY!
ROMPH!
YOU MUST GO SAVE WHAT'S RIGHTFULLY SANTA'S, UNCA DONALD! REMEMBER... YOU CAN COUNT ON THE MAIL SERVICE IN A PINCH!
I WISH I'D TAKEN A SAFER CHRISTMAS JOB... LIKE A-BOMB TESTER!
-GULP!- BE A SPORT, BARNEY! THAT PACKAGE ISN'T ADDRESSED TO "BEAR CLAUS"—
SNARLEDY-ROWR!
NO SENSE OF HUMOR! GRAB THE PACKAGE, KIDS!

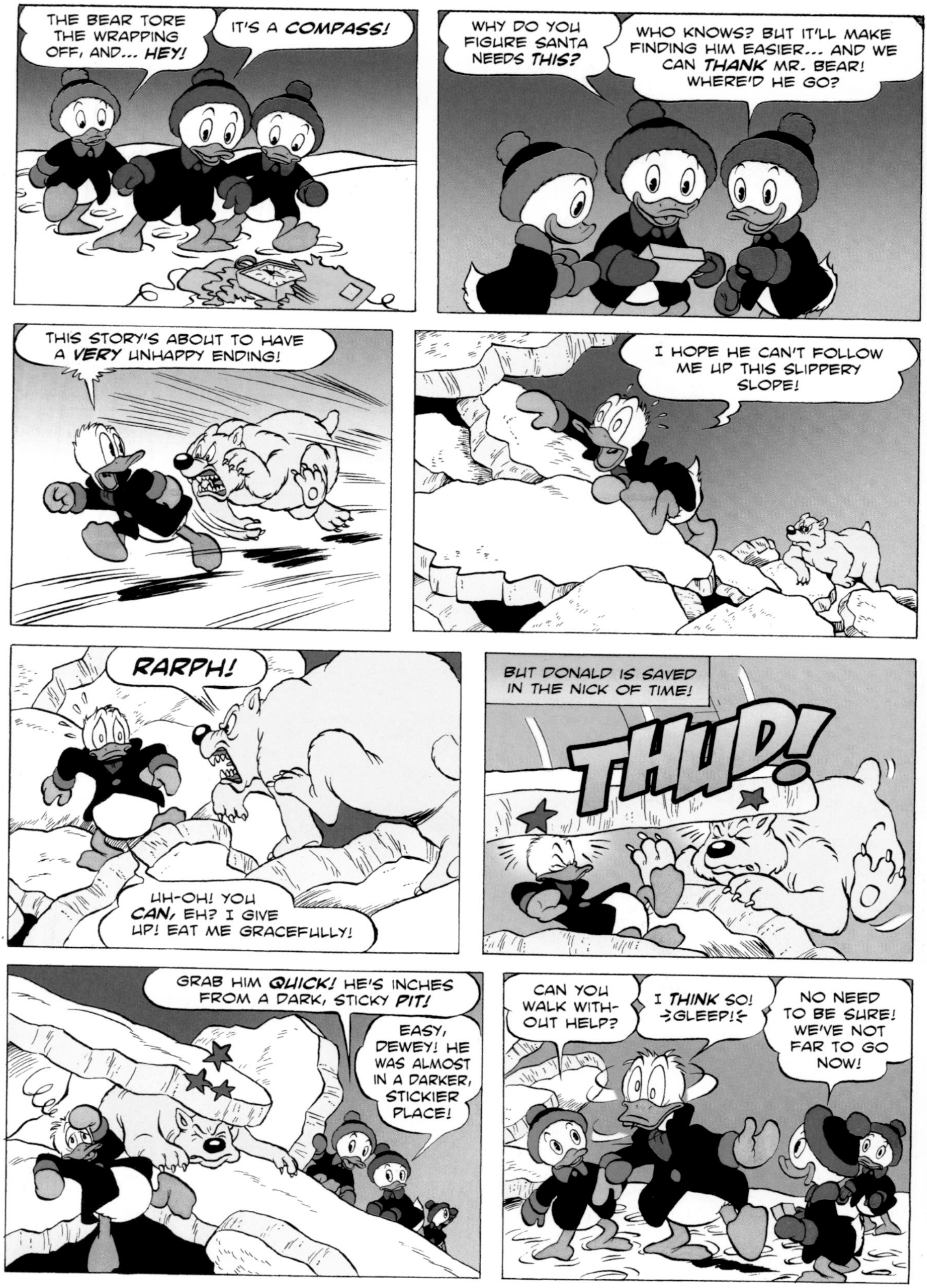
THE BEAR TORE THE WRAPPING OFF, AND... HEY!
IT'S A COMPASS!
WHY DO YOU FIGURE SANTA NEEDS THIS?
WHO KNOWS? BUT IT'LL MAKE FINDING HIM EASIER... AND WE CAN THANK MR. BEAR! WHERE'D HE GO?
THIS STORY'S ABOUT TO HAVE A VERY UNHAPPY ENDING!
I HOPE HE CAN'T FOLLOW ME UP THIS SLIPPERY SLOPE!
RARPH!
UH-OH! YOU CAN, EH? I GIVE UP! EAT ME GRACEFULLY!
BUT DONALD IS SAVED IN THE NICK OF TIME!
THUD!
GRAB HIM QUICK! HE'S INCHES FROM A DARK, STICKY PIT!
EASY, DEWEY! HE WAS ALMOST IN A DARKER, STICKIER PLACE!
CAN YOU WALK WITH-OUT HELP?
I THINK SO! GLEEP!
NO NEED TO BE SURE! WE'VE NOT FAR TO GO NOW!

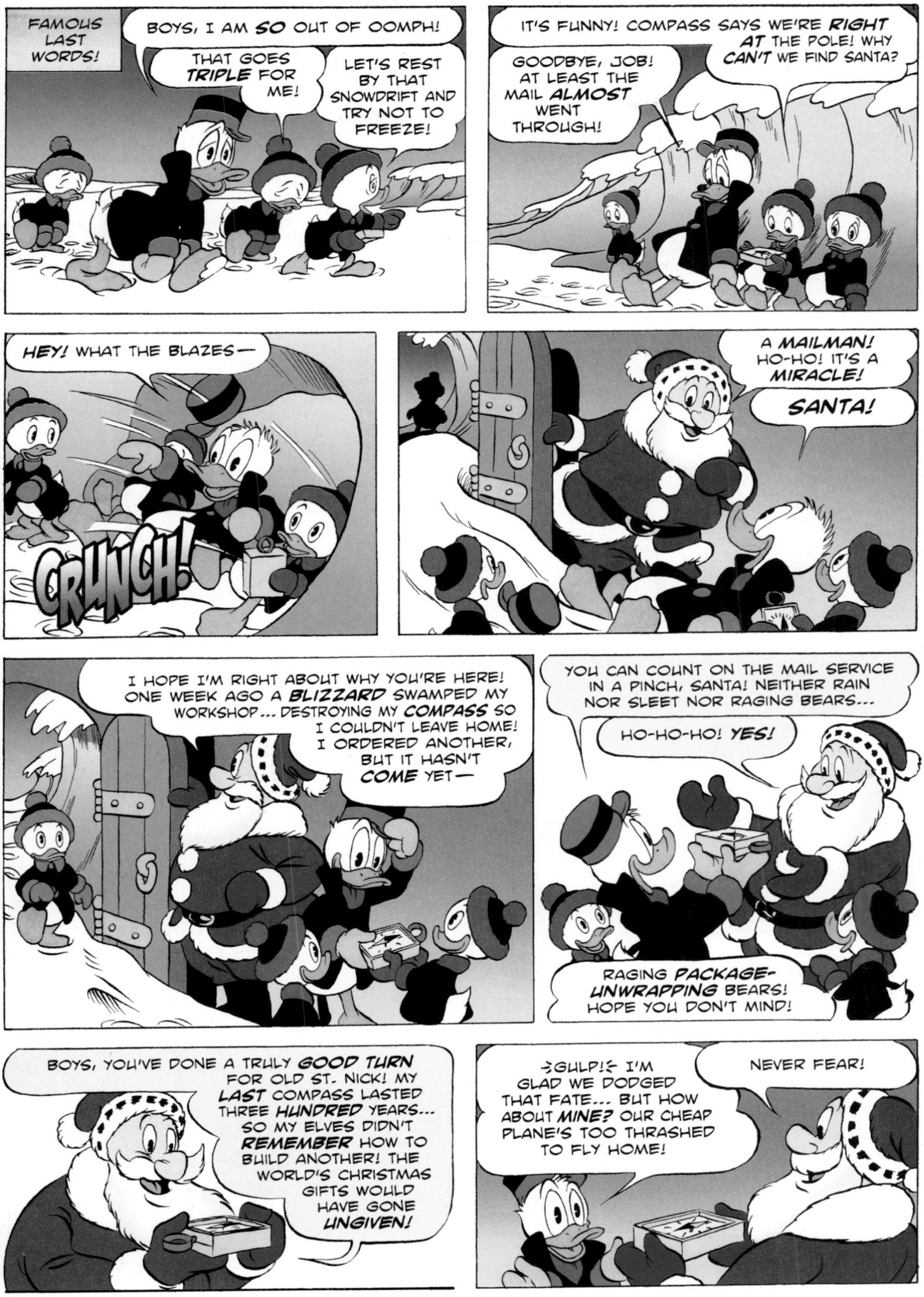
FAMOUS LAST WORDS!
BOYS, I AM SO OUT OF OOMPH!
THAT GOES TRIPLE FOR ME!
LET'S REST BY THAT SNOWDRIFT AND TRY NOT TO FREEZE!
IT'S FUNNY! COMPASS SAYS WE'RE RIGHT AT THE POLE! WHY CAN'T WE FIND SANTA?
GOODBYE, JOB! AT LEAST THE MAIL ALMOST WENT THROUGH!
HEY! WHAT THE BLAZES—
CRUNCH!
A MAILMAN! HO-HO! IT'S A MIRACLE!
SANTA!
I HOPE I'M RIGHT ABOUT WHY YOU'RE HERE! ONE WEEK AGO A BLIZZARD SWAMPED MY WORKSHOP... DESTROYING MY COMPASS SO I COULDN'T LEAVE HOME! I ORDERED ANOTHER, BUT IT HASN'T COME YET—
YOU CAN COUNT ON THE MAIL SERVICE IN A PINCH, SANTA! NEITHER RAIN NOR SLEET NOR RAGING BEARS...
HO-HO-HO! YES!
RAGING PACKAGE-UNWRAPPING BEARS! HOPE YOU DON'T MIND!
BOYS, YOU'VE DONE A TRULY GOOD TURN FOR OLD ST. NICK! MY LAST COMPASS LASTED THREE HUNDRED YEARS... SO MY ELVES DIDN'T REMEMBER HOW TO BUILD ANOTHER! THE WORLD'S CHRISTMAS GIFTS WOULD HAVE GONE UNGIVEN!
GULP! I'M GLAD WE DODGED THAT FATE... BUT HOW ABOUT MINE? OUR CHEAP PLANE'S TOO THRASHED TO FLY HOME!
NEVER FEAR!

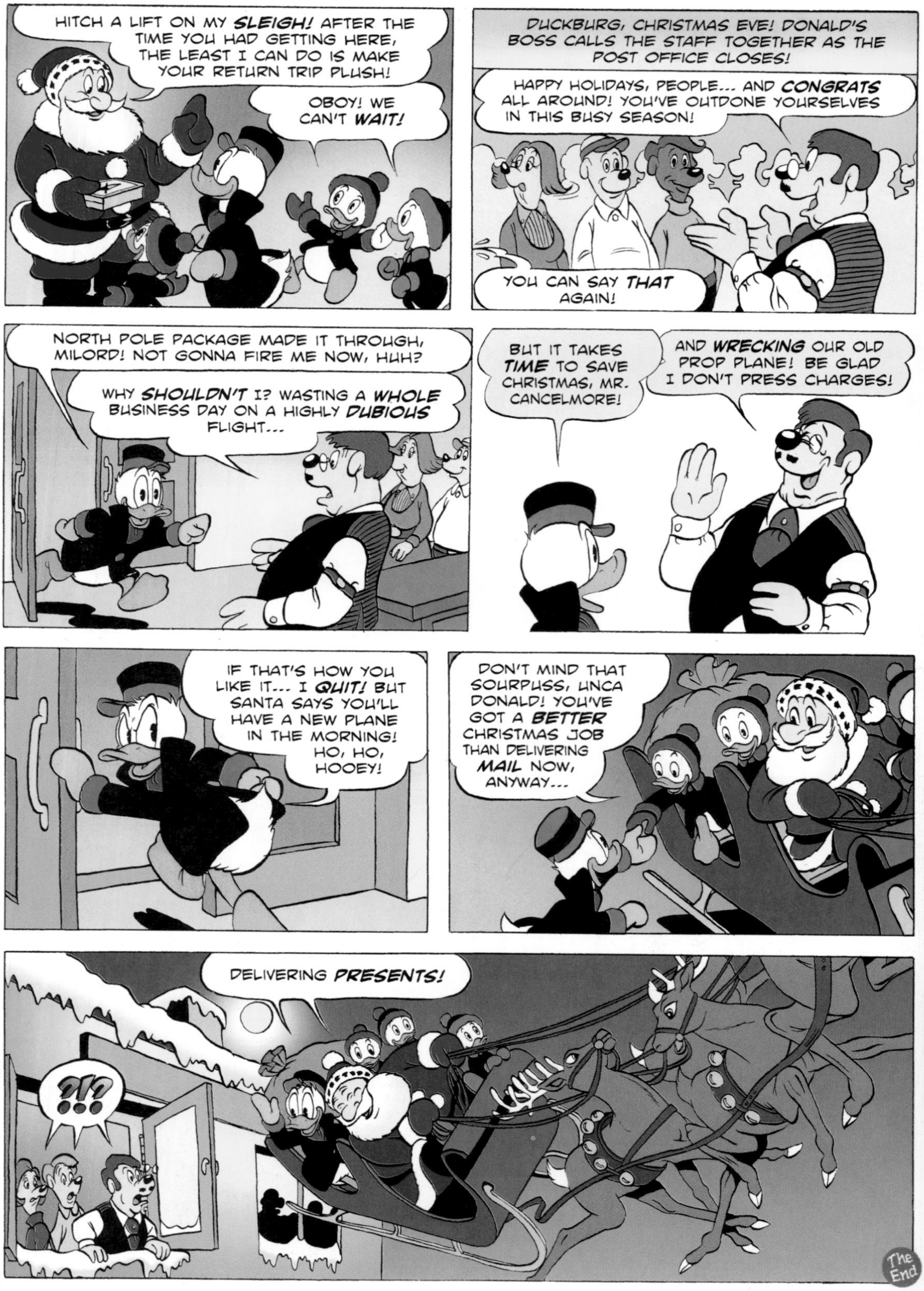
HITCH A LIFT ON MY SLEIGH! AFTER THE TIME YOU HAD GETTING HERE, THE LEAST I CAN DO IS MAKE YOUR RETURN TRIP PLUSH!
OBOY! WE CAN'T WAIT!
DUCKBURG, CHRISTMAS EVE! DONALD'S BOSS CALLS THE STAFF TOGETHER AS THE POST OFFICE CLOSES!
HAPPY HOLIDAYS, PEOPLE... AND CONGRATS ALL AROUND! YOU'VE OUTDONE YOURSELVES IN THIS BUSY SEASON!
YOU CAN SAY THAT AGAIN!
NORTH POLE PACKAGE MADE IT THROUGH, MILORD! NOT GONNA FIRE ME NOW, HUH?
WHY SHOULDN'T I? WASTING A WHOLE BUSINESS DAY ON A HIGHLY DUBIOUS FLIGHT...
BUT IT TAKES TIME TO SAVE CHRISTMAS, MR. CANCELMORE!
AND WRECKING OUR OLD PROP PLANE! BE GLAD I DON'T PRESS CHARGES!
IF THAT'S HOW YOU LIKE IT... I QUIT! BUT SANTA SAYS YOU'LL HAVE A NEW PLANE IN THE MORNING! HO, HO, HOOEY!
DON'T MIND THAT SOURPUSS, UNCA DONALD! YOU'VE GOT A BETTER CHRISTMAS JOB THAN DELIVERING MAIL NOW, ANYWAY...
DELIVERING PRESENTS!
?!?
The End

Walt Disney's Mickey Mouse in Claws of the Cat

- PART 1 -

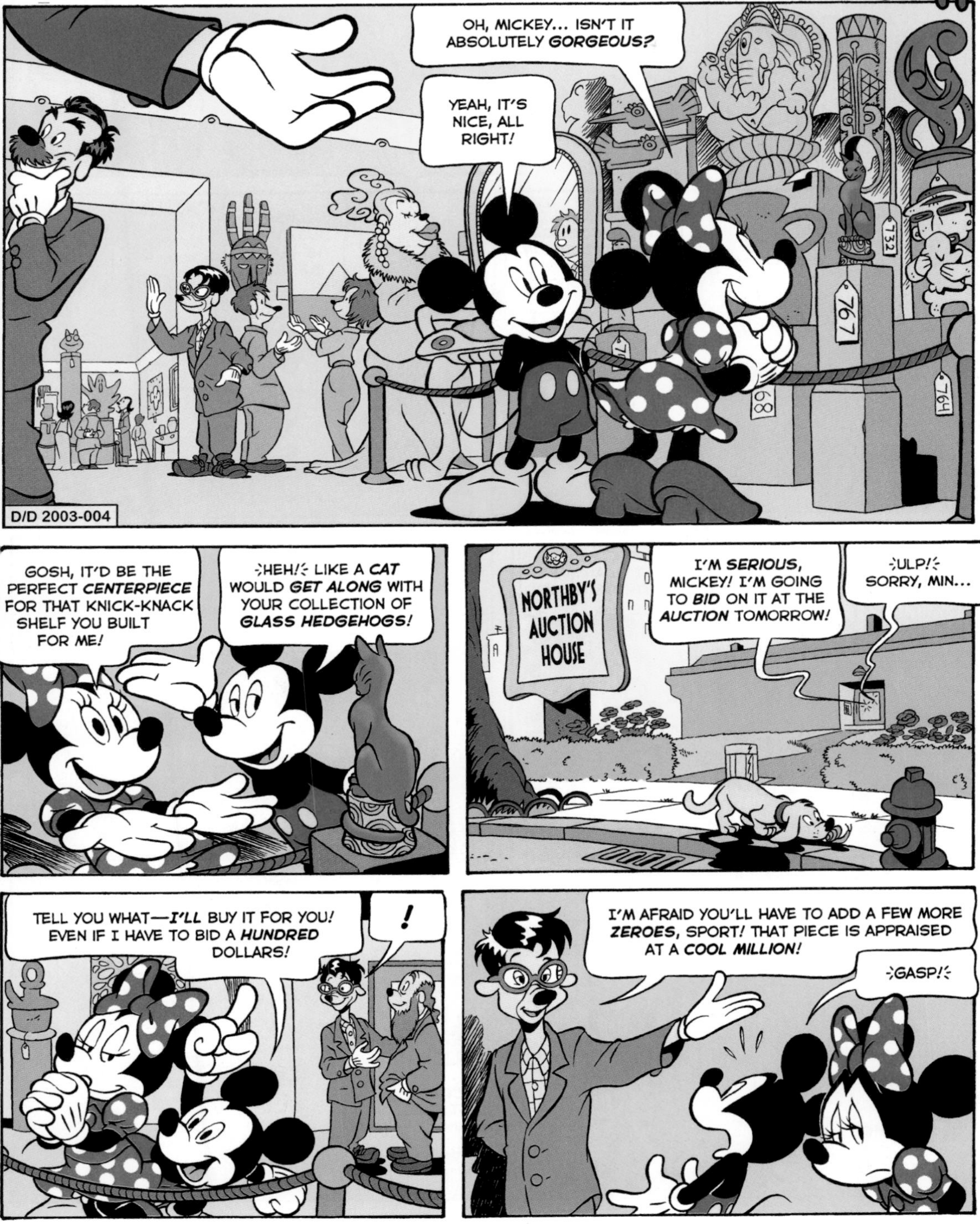

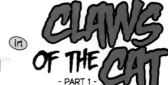

OH, MICKEY... ISN'T IT ABSOLUTELY GORGEOUS?
YEAH, IT'S NICE, ALL RIGHT!
767
764
732
D/D 2003-004
GOSH, IT'D BE THE PERFECT CENTERPIECE FOR THAT KNICK-KNACK SHELF YOU BUILT FOR ME!
HEH! LIKE A CAT WOULD GET ALONG WITH YOUR COLLECTION OF GLASS HEDGEHOGS!
NORTHBY'S AUCTION HOUSE
I'M SERIOUS, MICKEY! I'M GOING TO BID ON IT AT THE AUCTION TOMORROW!
ULP! SORRY, MIN...
TELL YOU WHAT—I'LL BUY IT FOR YOU! EVEN IF I HAVE TO BID A HUNDRED DOLLARS!
!
I'M AFRAID YOU'LL HAVE TO ADD A FEW MORE ZEROES, SPORT! THAT PIECE IS APPRAISED AT A COOL MILLION!
GASP!

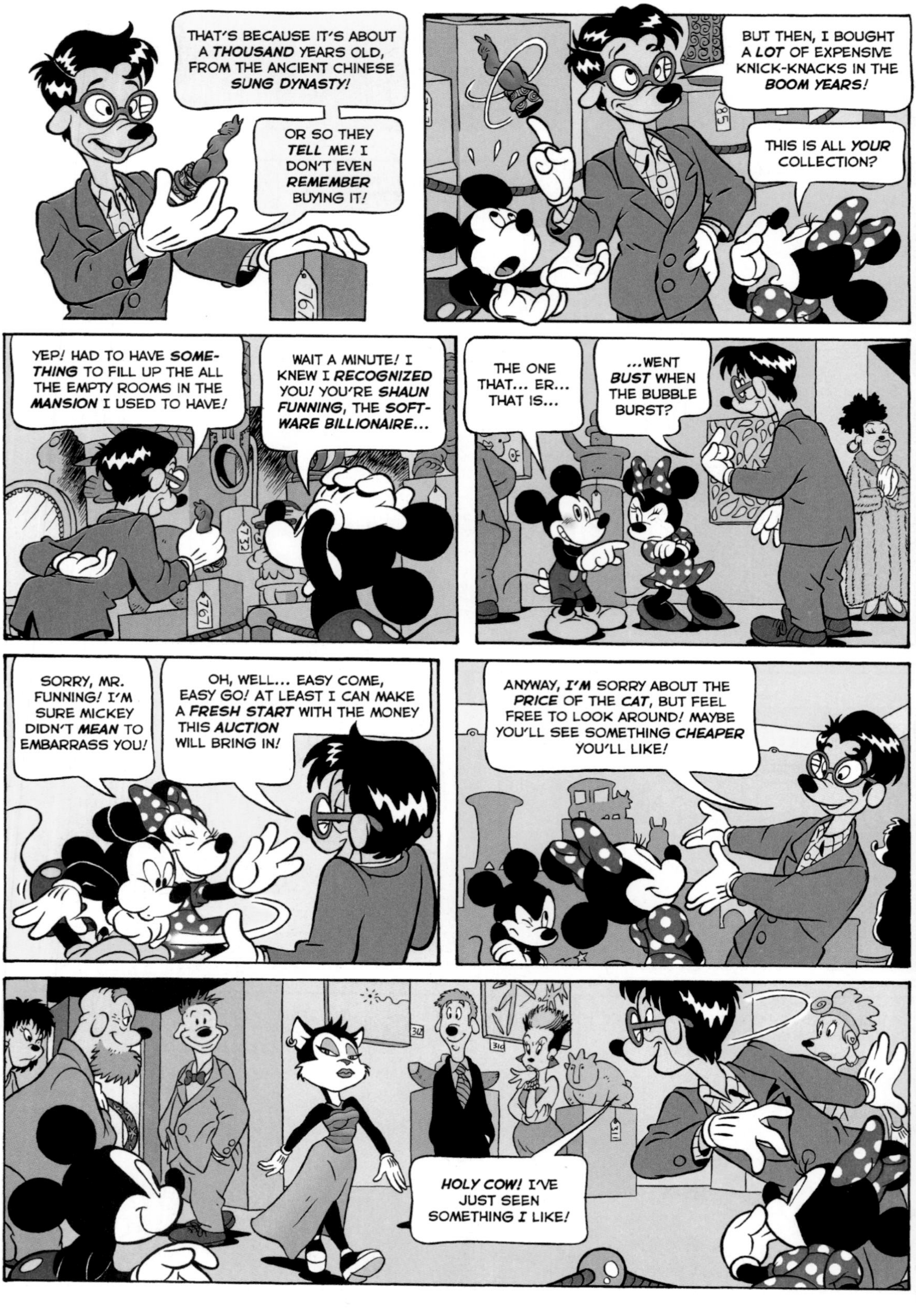
THAT'S BECAUSE IT'S ABOUT A THOUSAND YEARS OLD, FROM THE ANCIENT CHINESE SUNG DYNASTY!
OR SO THEY TELL ME! I DON'T EVEN REMEMBER BUYING IT!
767
BUT THEN, I BOUGHT A LOT OF EXPENSIVE KNICK-KNACKS IN THE BOOM YEARS!
THIS IS ALL YOUR COLLECTION?
785
YEP! HAD TO HAVE SOMETHING TO FILL UP THE ALL THE EMPTY ROOMS IN THE MANSION I USED TO HAVE!
WAIT A MINUTE! I KNEW I RECOGNIZED YOU! YOU'RE SHAUN FUNNING, THE SOFTWARE BILLIONAIRE...
732
767
THE ONE THAT... ER... THAT IS...
...WENT BUST WHEN THE BUBBLE BURST?
SORRY, MR. FUNNING! I'M SURE MICKEY DIDN'T MEAN TO EMBARRASS YOU!
OH, WELL... EASY COME, EASY GO! AT LEAST I CAN MAKE A FRESH START WITH THE MONEY THIS AUCTION WILL BRING IN!
ANYWAY, I'M SORRY ABOUT THE PRICE OF THE CAT, BUT FEEL FREE TO LOOK AROUND! MAYBE YOU'LL SEE SOMETHING CHEAPER YOU'LL LIKE!
312
310
311
HOLY COW! I'VE JUST SEEN SOMETHING I LIKE!

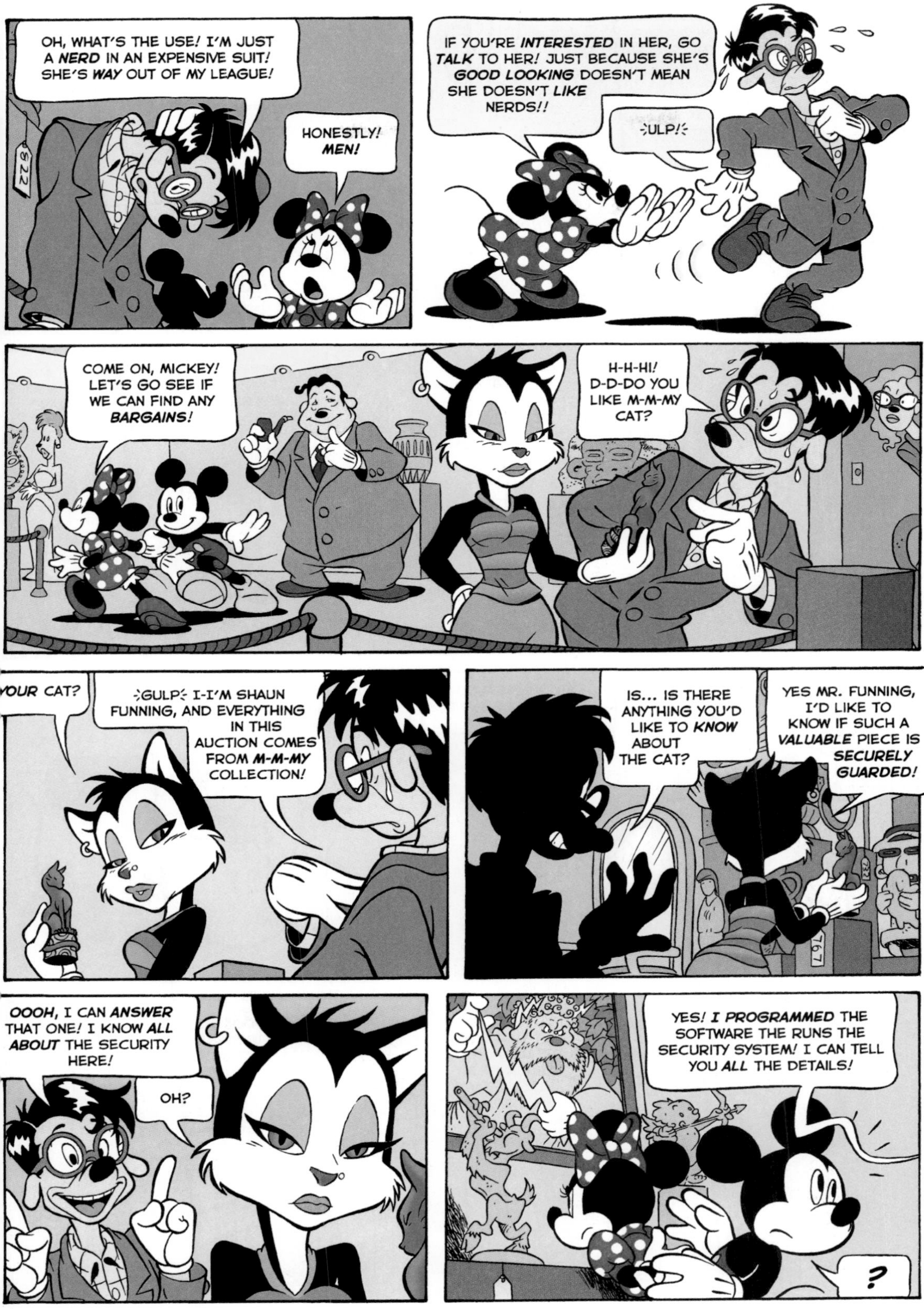
OH, WHAT'S THE USE! I'M JUST A NERD IN AN EXPENSIVE SUIT! SHE'S WAY OUT OF MY LEAGUE!
822
HONESTLY! MEN!
IF YOU'RE INTERESTED IN HER, GO TALK TO HER! JUST BECAUSE SHE'S GOOD LOOKING DOESN'T MEAN SHE DOESN'T LIKE NERDS!!
ULP!
COME ON, MICKEY! LET'S GO SEE IF WE CAN FIND ANY BARGAINS!
H-H-HI! D-D-DO YOU LIKE M-M-MY CAT?
YOUR CAT?
GULP I-I'M SHAUN FUNNING, AND EVERYTHING IN THIS AUCTION COMES FROM M-M-MY COLLECTION!
IS... IS THERE ANYTHING YOU'D LIKE TO KNOW ABOUT THE CAT?
YES MR. FUNNING, I'D LIKE TO KNOW IF SUCH A VALUABLE PIECE IS SECURELY GUARDED!
OOOH, I CAN ANSWER THAT ONE! I KNOW ALL ABOUT THE SECURITY HERE!
OH?
YES! I PROGRAMMED THE SOFTWARE THE RUNS THE SECURITY SYSTEM! I CAN TELL YOU ALL THE DETAILS!
?

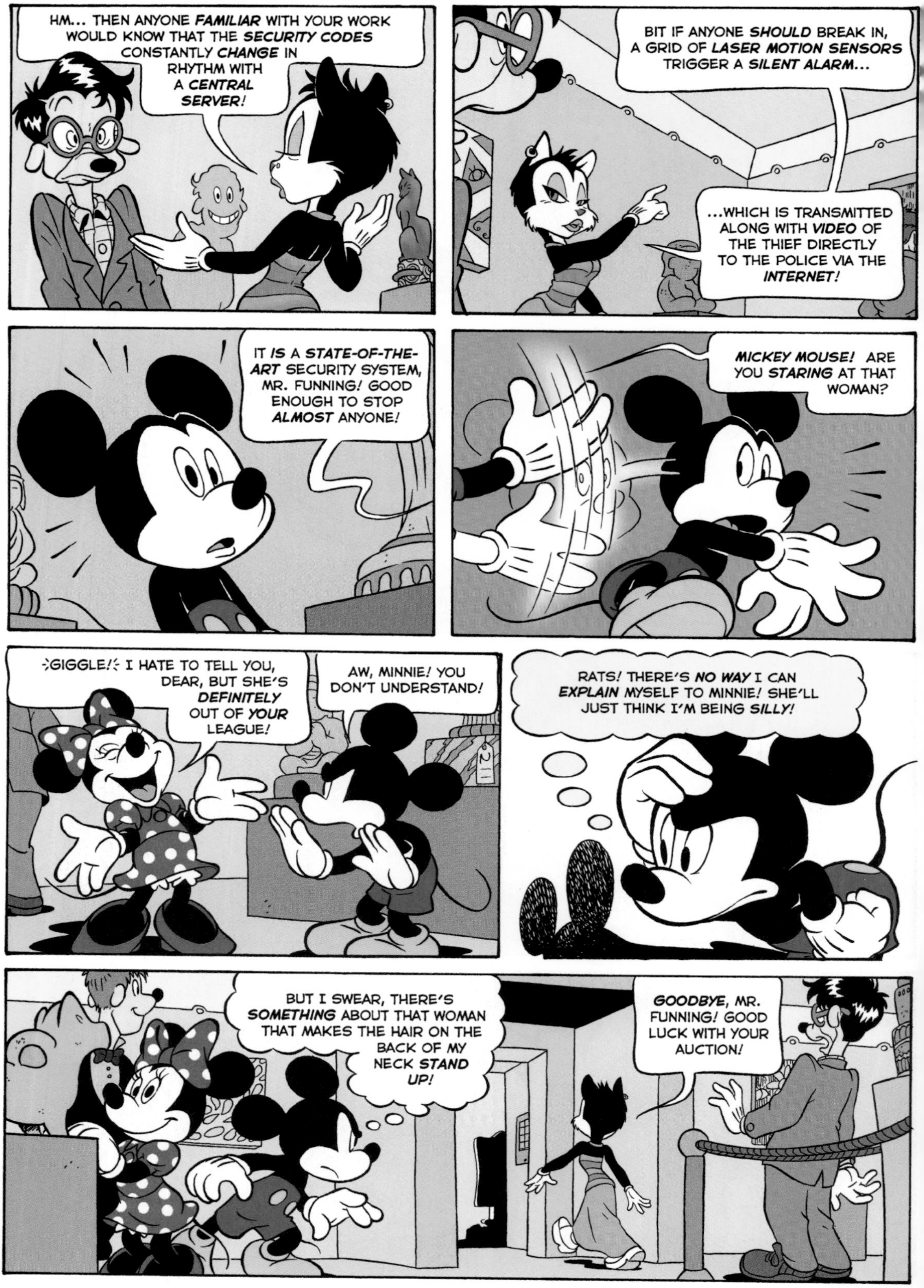
HM... THEN ANYONE FAMILIAR WITH YOUR WORK WOULD KNOW THAT THE SECURITY CODES CONSTANTLY CHANGE IN RHYTHM WITH A CENTRAL SERVER!
BIT IF ANYONE SHOULD BREAK IN, A GRID OF LASER MOTION SENSORS TRIGGER A SILENT ALARM...
...WHICH IS TRANSMITTED ALONG WITH VIDEO OF THE THIEF DIRECTLY TO THE POLICE VIA THE INTERNET!
IT IS A STATE-OF-THE-ART SECURITY SYSTEM, MR. FUNNING! GOOD ENOUGH TO STOP ALMOST ANYONE!
MICKEY MOUSE! ARE YOU STARING AT THAT WOMAN?
GIGGLE! I HATE TO TELL YOU, DEAR, BUT SHE'S DEFINITELY OUT OF YOUR LEAGUE!
AW, MINNIE! YOU DON'T UNDERSTAND!
RATS! THERE'S NO WAY I CAN EXPLAIN MYSELF TO MINNIE! SHE'LL JUST THINK I'M BEING SILLY!
BUT I SWEAR, THERE'S SOMETHING ABOUT THAT WOMAN THAT MAKES THE HAIR ON THE BACK OF MY NECK STAND UP!
GOODBYE, MR. FUNNING! GOOD LUCK WITH YOUR AUCTION!

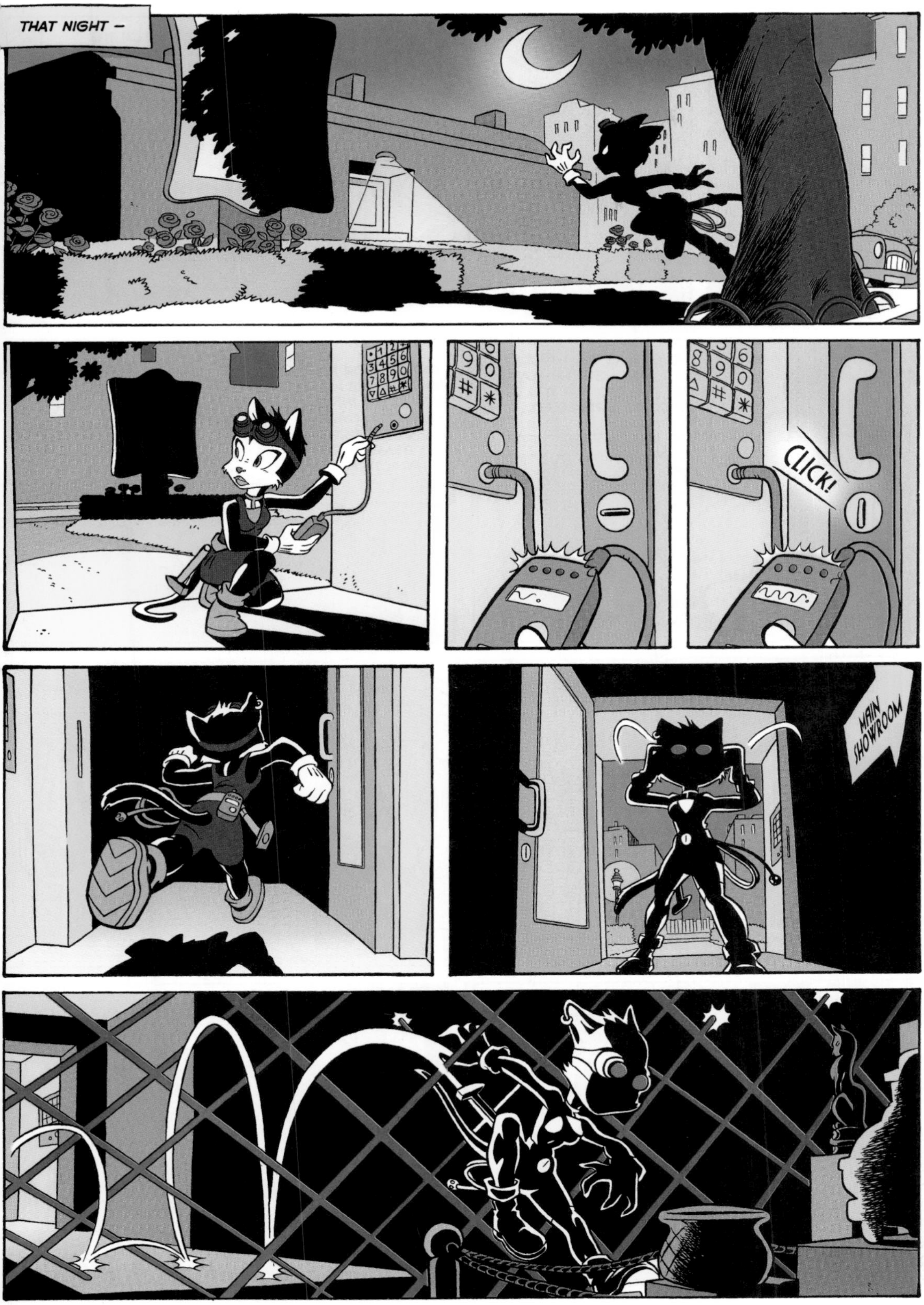
THAT NIGHT —
CLICK!
MAIN SHOWROOM

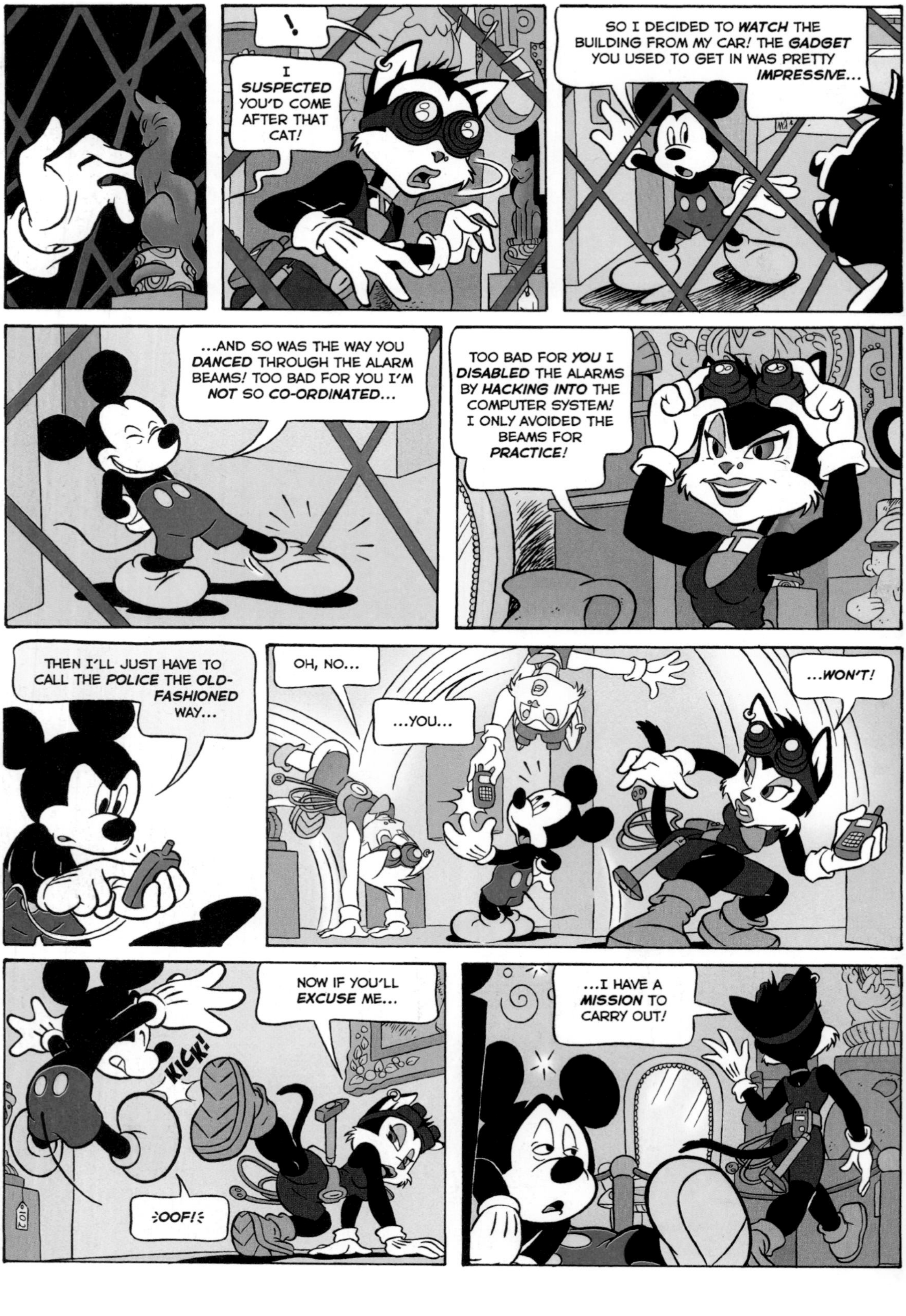
!
I SUSPECTED YOU'D COME AFTER THAT CAT!
SO I DECIDED TO WATCH THE BUILDING FROM MY CAR! THE GADGET YOU USED TO GET IN WAS PRETTY IMPRESSIVE...
...AND SO WAS THE WAY YOU DANCED THROUGH THE ALARM BEAMS! TOO BAD FOR YOU I'M NOT SO CO-ORDINATED...
TOO BAD FOR YOU I DISABLED THE ALARMS BY HACKING INTO THE COMPUTER SYSTEM! I ONLY AVOIDED THE BEAMS FOR PRACTICE!
THEN I'LL JUST HAVE TO CALL THE POLICE THE OLD-FASHIONED WAY...
OH, NO...
...YOU...
...WON'T!
NOW IF YOU'LL EXCUSE ME...
KICK!
OOF!
...I HAVE A MISSION TO CARRY OUT!

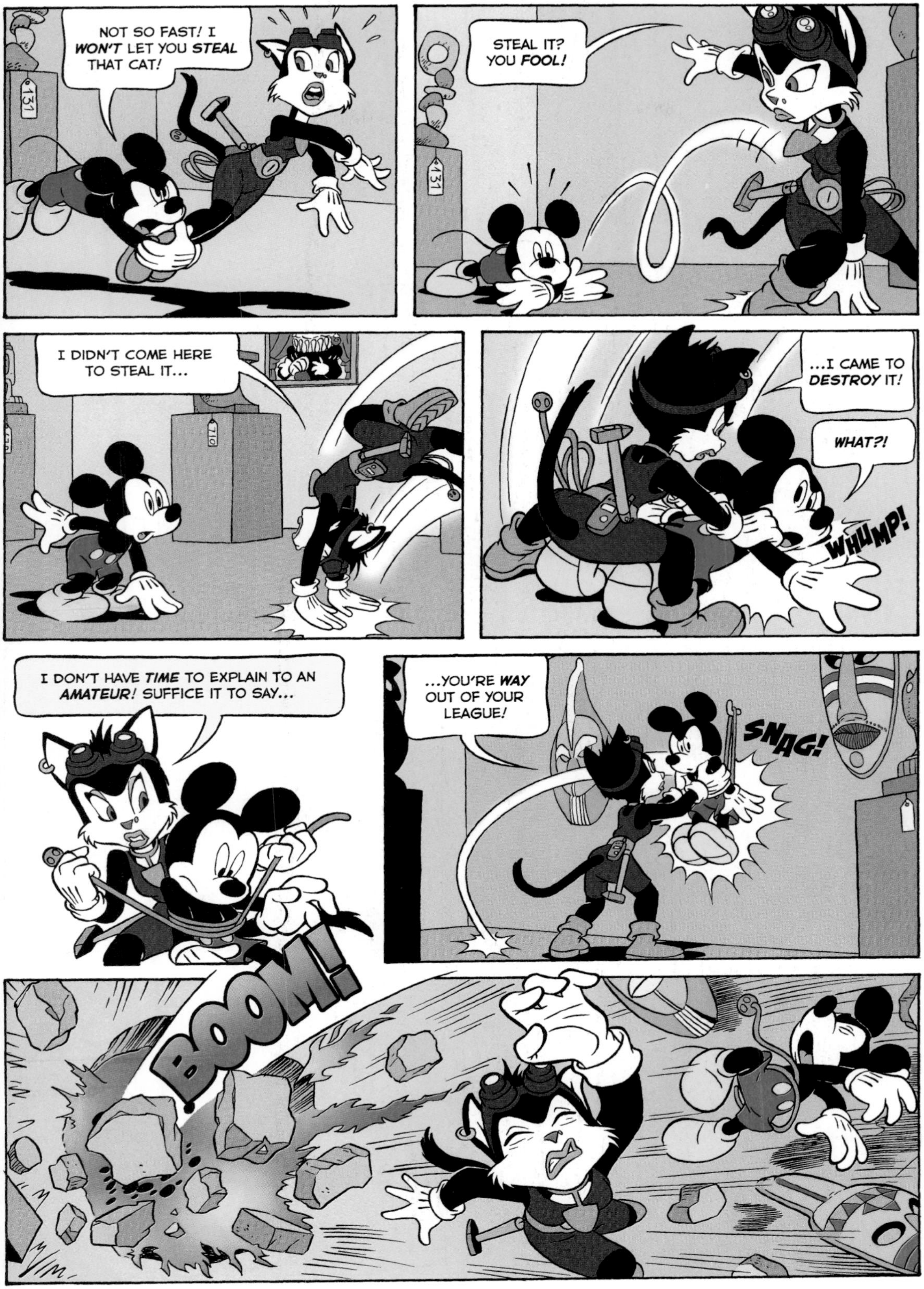
NOT SO FAST! I WON'T LET YOU STEAL THAT CAT!
131
STEAL IT? YOU FOOL!
131
I DIDN'T COME HERE TO STEAL IT...
...I CAME TO DESTROY IT!
WHAT?!
WHUMP!
I DON'T HAVE TIME TO EXPLAIN TO AN AMATEUR! SUFFICE IT TO SAY...
...YOU'RE WAY OUT OF YOUR LEAGUE!
SNAG!
BOOM!!

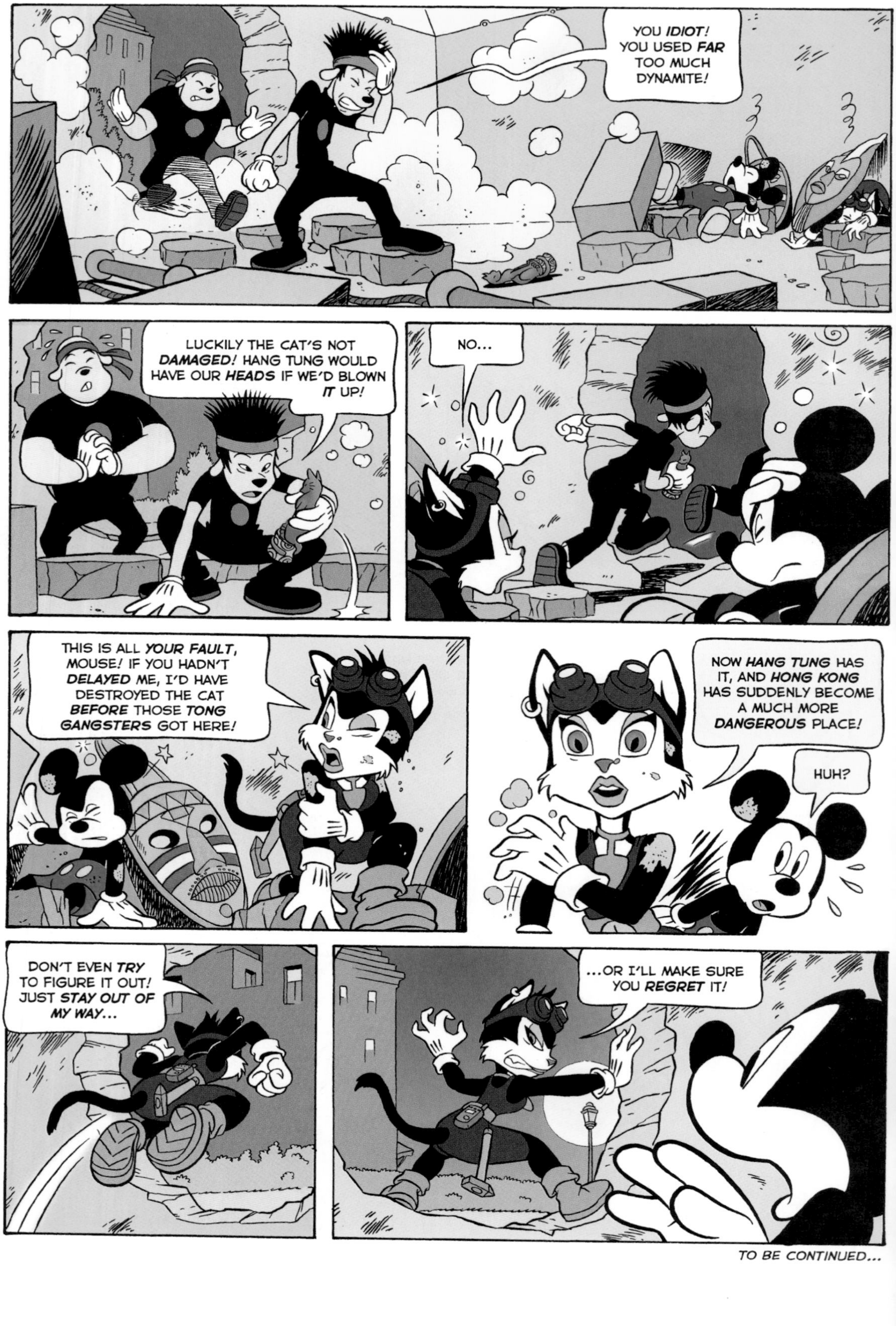
YOU IDIOT! YOU USED FAR TOO MUCH DYNAMITE!
LUCKILY THE CAT'S NOT DAMAGED! HANG TUNG WOULD HAVE OUR HEADS IF WE'D BLOWN IT UP!
NO...
THIS IS ALL YOUR FAULT, MOUSE! IF YOU HADN'T DELAYED ME, I'D HAVE DESTROYED THE CAT BEFORE THOSE TONG GANGSTERS GOT HERE!
NOW HANG TUNG HAS IT, AND HONG KONG HAS SUDDENLY BECOME A MUCH MORE DANGEROUS PLACE!
HUH?
DON'T EVEN TRY TO FIGURE IT OUT! JUST STAY OUT OF MY WAY...
...OR I'LL MAKE SURE YOU REGRET IT!

TO BE CONTINUED...

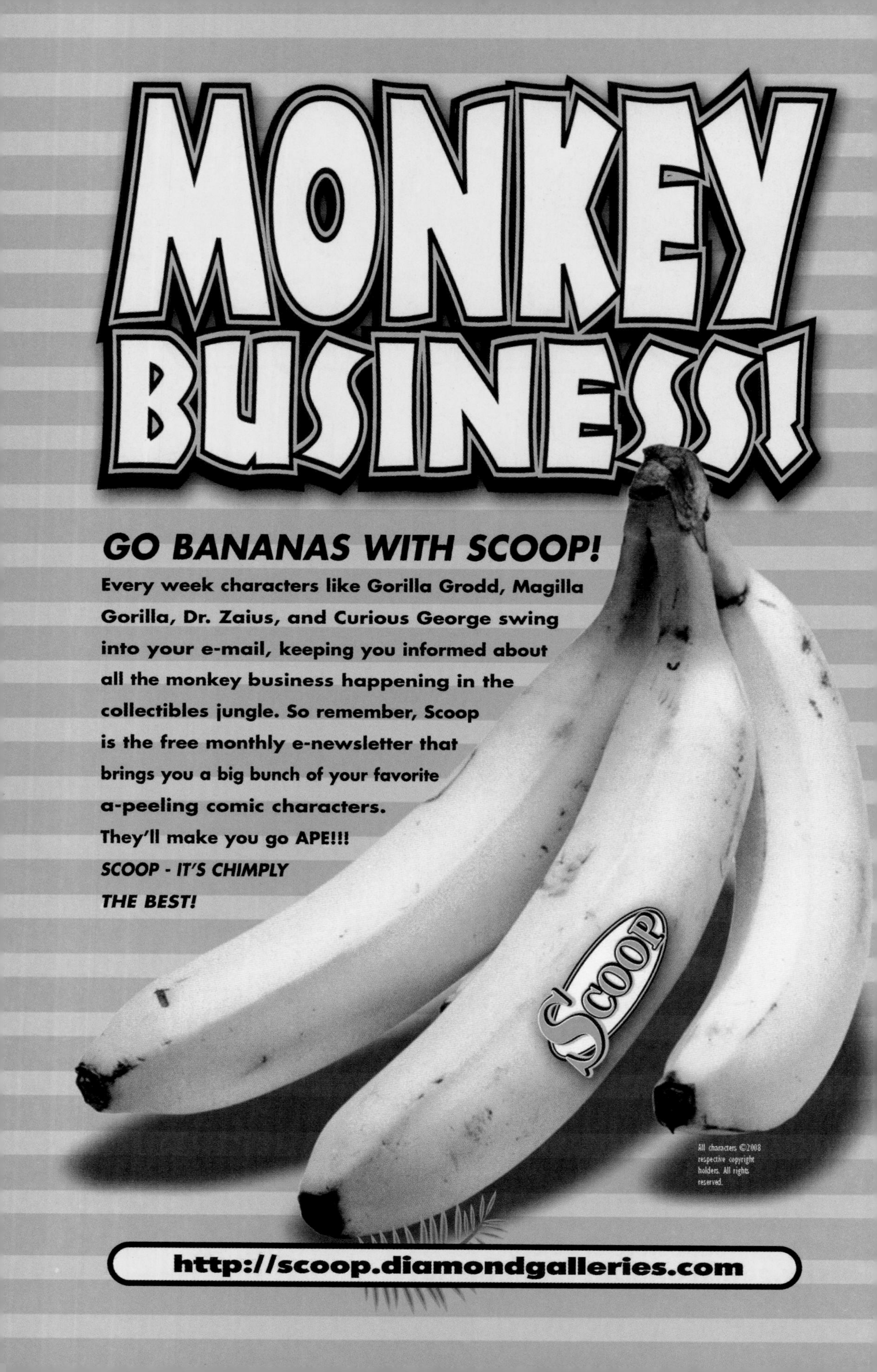
MONKEY BUSINESS!
GO BANANAS WITH SCOOP!
Every week characters like Gorilla Grodd, Magilla Gorilla, Dr. Zaius, and Curious George swing into your e-mail, keeping you informed about all the monkey business happening in the collectibles jungle. So remember, Scoop is the free monthly e-newsletter that brings you a big bunch of your favorite a-peeling comic characters.
They'll make you go APE!!!
SCOOP - IT'S CHIMPLY THE BEST!
Scoop
All characters ©2008 respective copyright holders. All rights reserved.
http://scoop.diamondgalleries.com

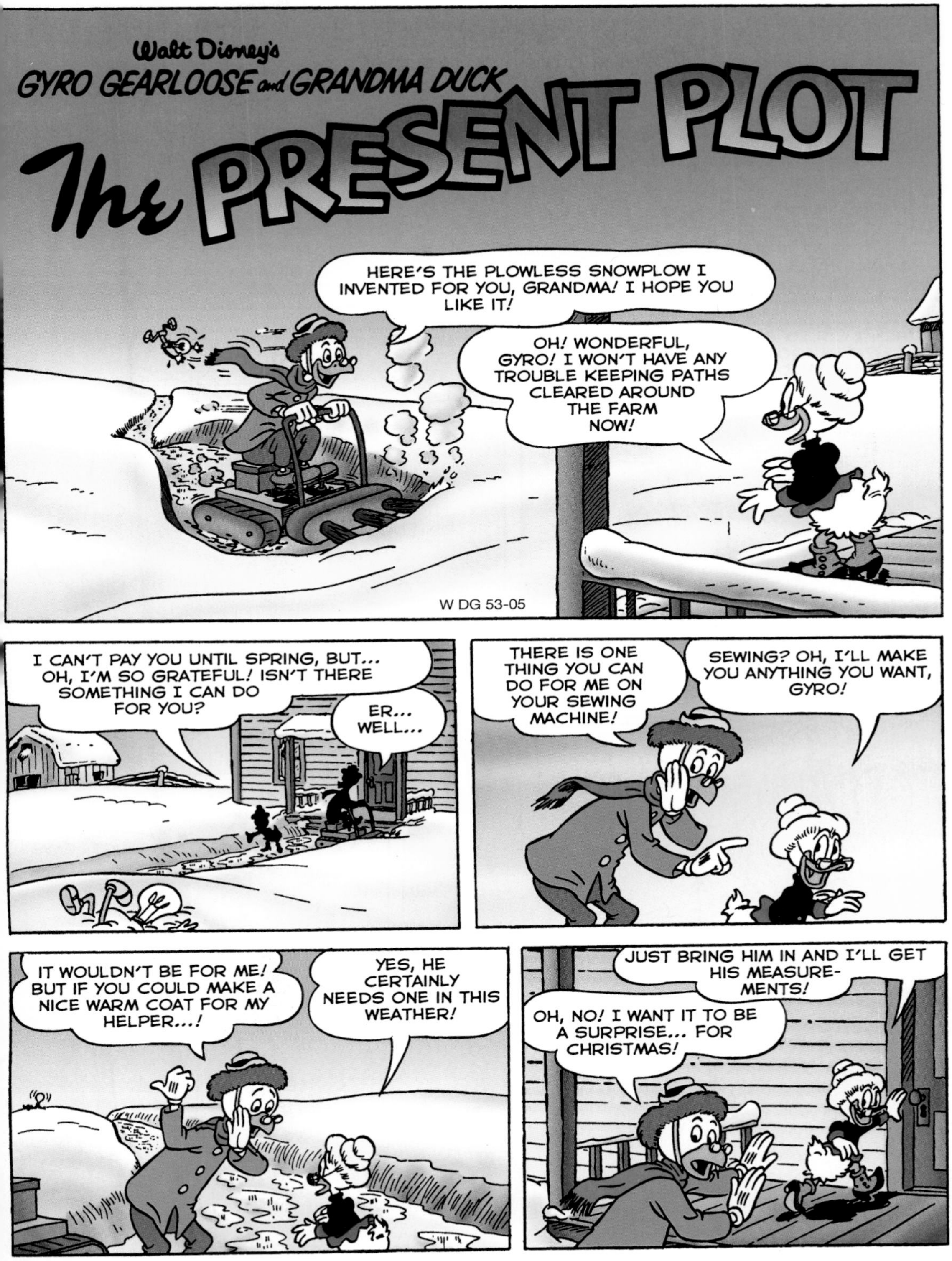
Walt Disney's
GYRO GEARLOOSE and GRANDMA DUCK
The PRESENT PLOT
HERE'S THE PLOWLESS SNOWPLOW I INVENTED FOR YOU, GRANDMA! I HOPE YOU LIKE IT!
OH! WONDERFUL, GYRO! I WON'T HAVE ANY TROUBLE KEEPING PATHS CLEARED AROUND THE FARM NOW!
W DG 53-05
I CAN'T PAY YOU UNTIL SPRING, BUT... OH, I'M SO GRATEFUL! ISN'T THERE SOMETHING I CAN DO FOR YOU?
ER... WELL...
THERE IS ONE THING YOU CAN DO FOR ME ON YOUR SEWING MACHINE!
SEWING? OH, I'LL MAKE YOU ANYTHING YOU WANT, GYRO!
IT WOULDN'T BE FOR ME! BUT IF YOU COULD MAKE A NICE WARM COAT FOR MY HELPER...!
YES, HE CERTAINLY NEEDS ONE IN THIS WEATHER!
JUST BRING HIM IN AND I'LL GET HIS MEASURE-MENTS!
OH, NO! I WANT IT TO BE A SURPRISE... FOR CHRISTMAS!

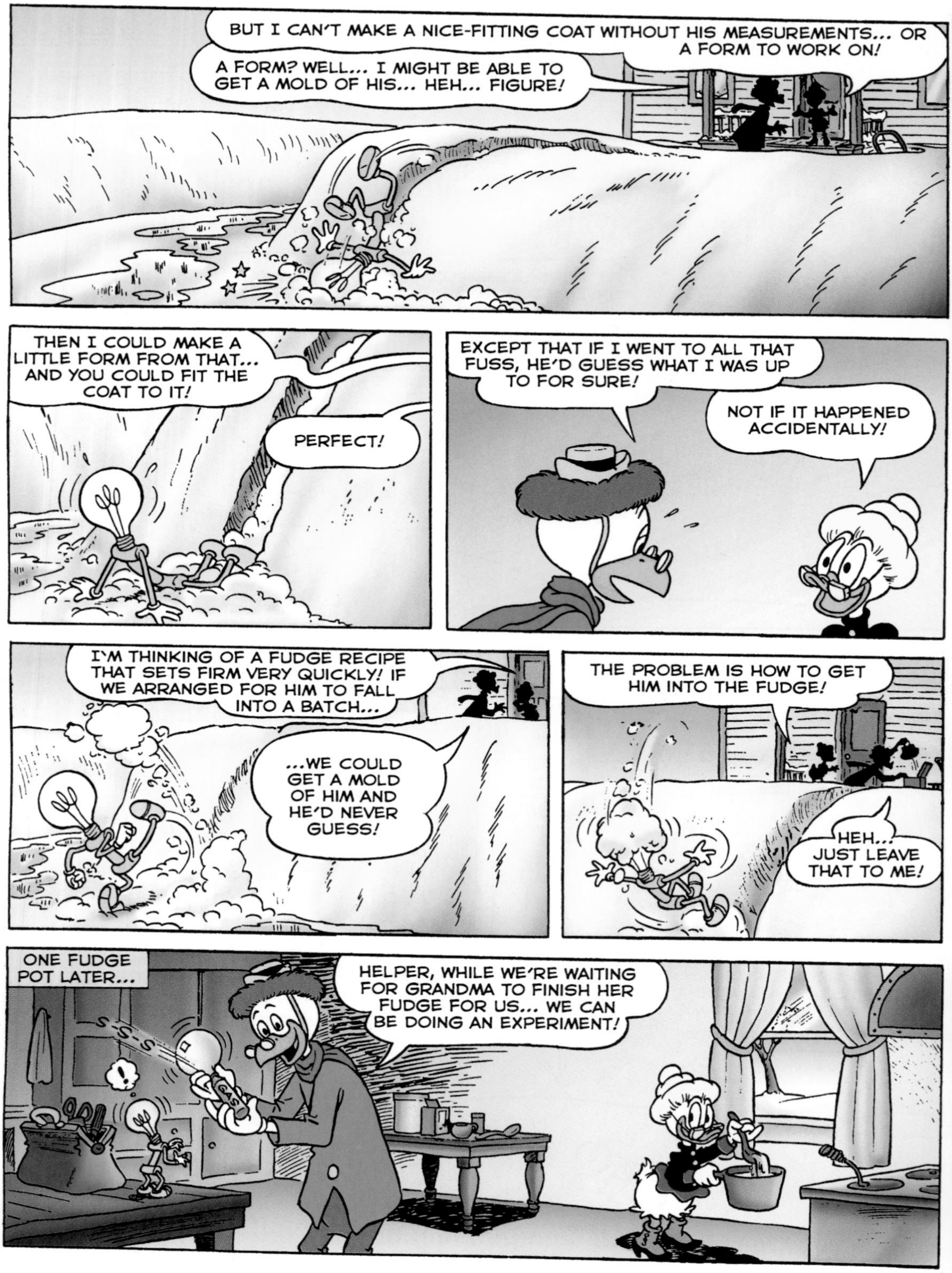
BUT I CAN'T MAKE A NICE-FITTING COAT WITHOUT HIS MEASUREMENTS... OR A FORM TO WORK ON!
A FORM? WELL... I MIGHT BE ABLE TO GET A MOLD OF HIS... HEH... FIGURE!
THEN I COULD MAKE A LITTLE FORM FROM THAT... AND YOU COULD FIT THE COAT TO IT!
PERFECT!
EXCEPT THAT IF I WENT TO ALL THAT FUSS, HE'D GUESS WHAT I WAS UP TO FOR SURE!
NOT IF IT HAPPENED ACCIDENTALLY!
I'M THINKING OF A FUDGE RECIPE THAT SETS FIRM VERY QUICKLY! IF WE ARRANGED FOR HIM TO FALL INTO A BATCH...
...WE COULD GET A MOLD OF HIM AND HE'D NEVER GUESS!
THE PROBLEM IS HOW TO GET HIM INTO THE FUDGE!
HEH... JUST LEAVE THAT TO ME!
ONE FUDGE POT LATER...
HELPER, WHILE WE'RE WAITING FOR GRANDMA TO FINISH HER FUDGE FOR US... WE CAN BE DOING AN EXPERIMENT!
S-S-S
GAS

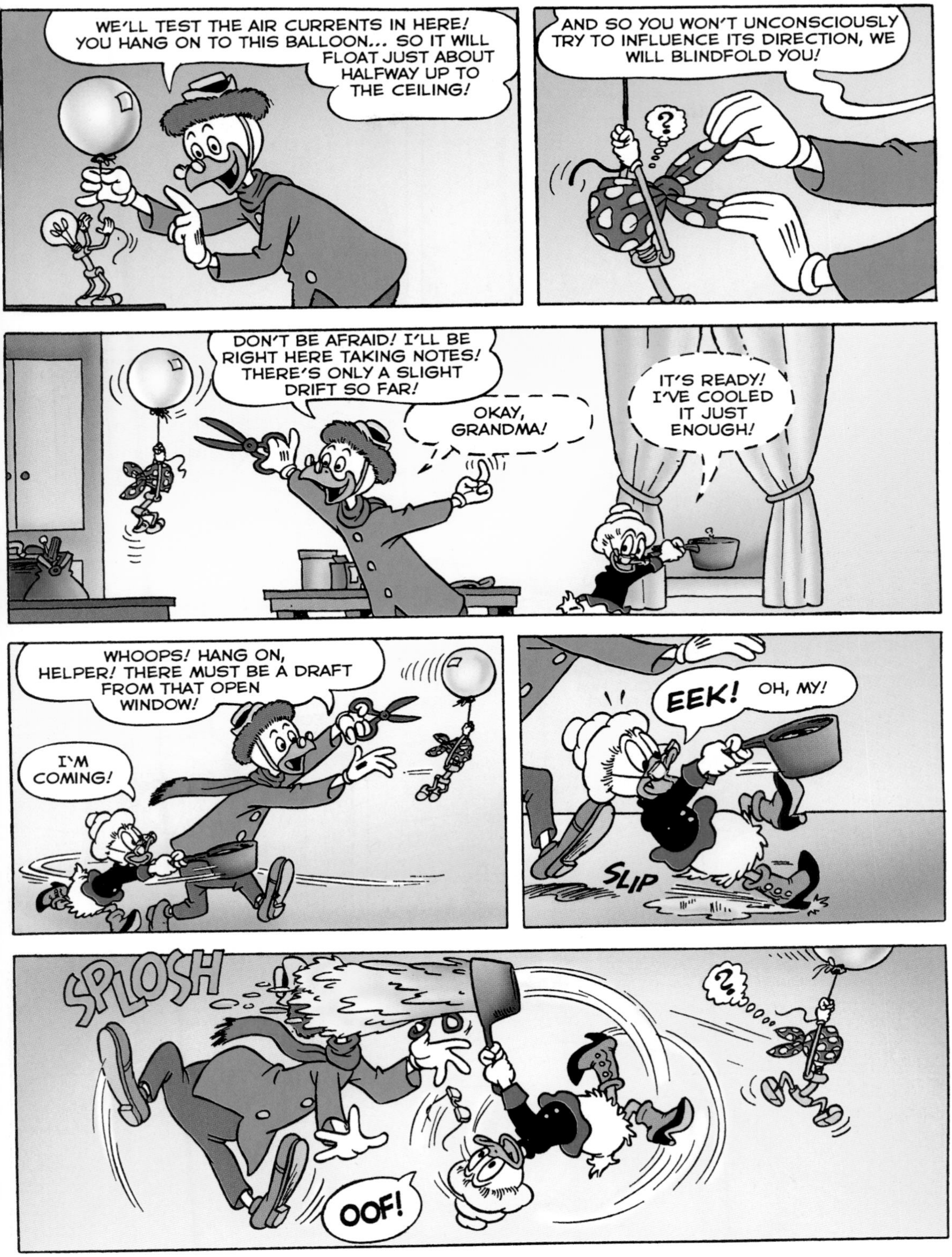
WE'LL TEST THE AIR CURRENTS IN HERE! YOU HANG ON TO THIS BALLOON... SO IT WILL FLOAT JUST ABOUT HALFWAY UP TO THE CEILING!
AND SO YOU WON'T UNCONSCIOUSLY TRY TO INFLUENCE ITS DIRECTION, WE WILL BLINDFOLD YOU!
?
DON'T BE AFRAID! I'LL BE RIGHT HERE TAKING NOTES! THERE'S ONLY A SLIGHT DRIFT SO FAR!
OKAY, GRANDMA!
IT'S READY! I'VE COOLED IT JUST ENOUGH!
WHOOPS! HANG ON, HELPER! THERE MUST BE A DRAFT FROM THAT OPEN WINDOW!
I'M COMING!
EEK!
OH, MY!
SLIP
SPLOSH
?
OOF!

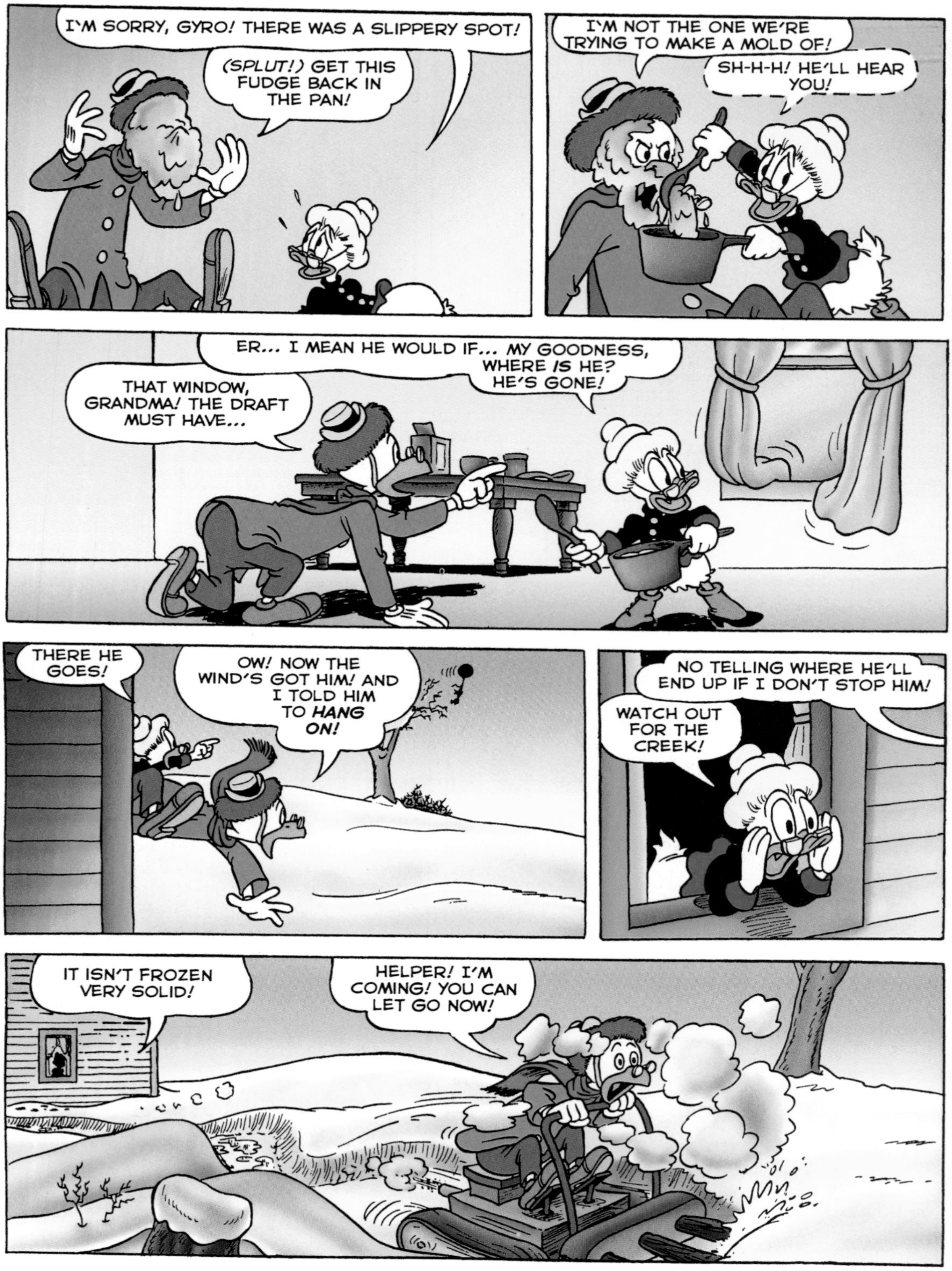
I'M SORRY, GYRO! THERE WAS A SLIPPERY SPOT!
(SPLUT!) GET THIS FUDGE BACK IN THE PAN!
I'M NOT THE ONE WE'RE TRYING TO MAKE A MOLD OF!
SH-H-H! HE'LL HEAR YOU!
ER... I MEAN HE WOULD IF... MY GOODNESS, WHERE IS HE? HE'S GONE!
THAT WINDOW, GRANDMA! THE DRAFT MUST HAVE...
THERE HE GOES!
OW! NOW THE WIND'S GOT HIM! AND I TOLD HIM TO HANG ON!
NO TELLING WHERE HE'LL END UP IF I DON'T STOP HIM!
WATCH OUT FOR THE CREEK!
IT ISN'T FROZEN VERY SOLID!
HELPER! I'M COMING! YOU CAN LET GO NOW!

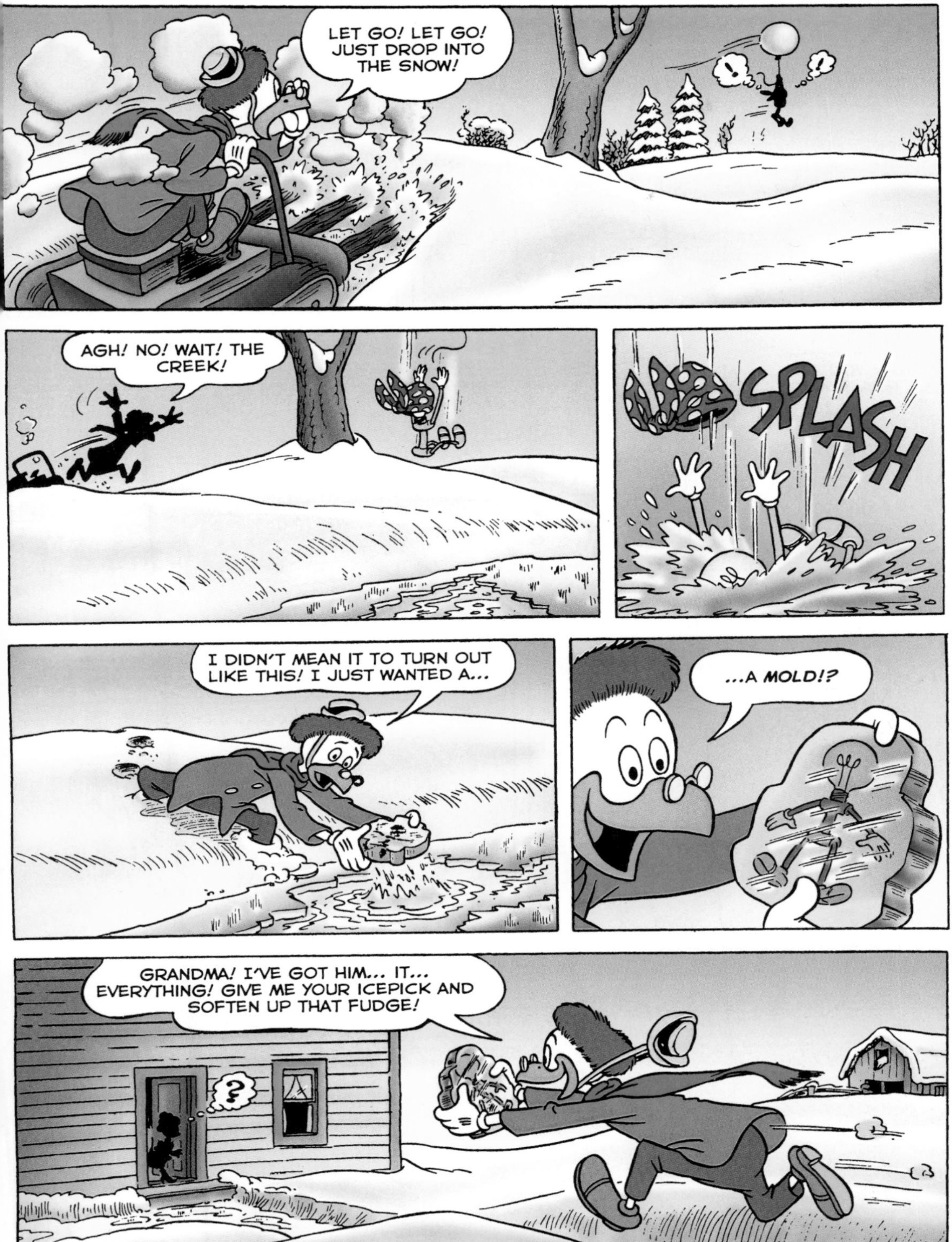
LET GO! LET GO! JUST DROP INTO THE SNOW!
AGH! NO! WAIT! THE CREEK!
SPLASH
I DIDN'T MEAN IT TO TURN OUT LIKE THIS! I JUST WANTED A...
...A MOLD!?
GRANDMA! I'VE GOT HIM... IT... EVERYTHING! GIVE ME YOUR ICEPICK AND SOFTEN UP THAT FUDGE!

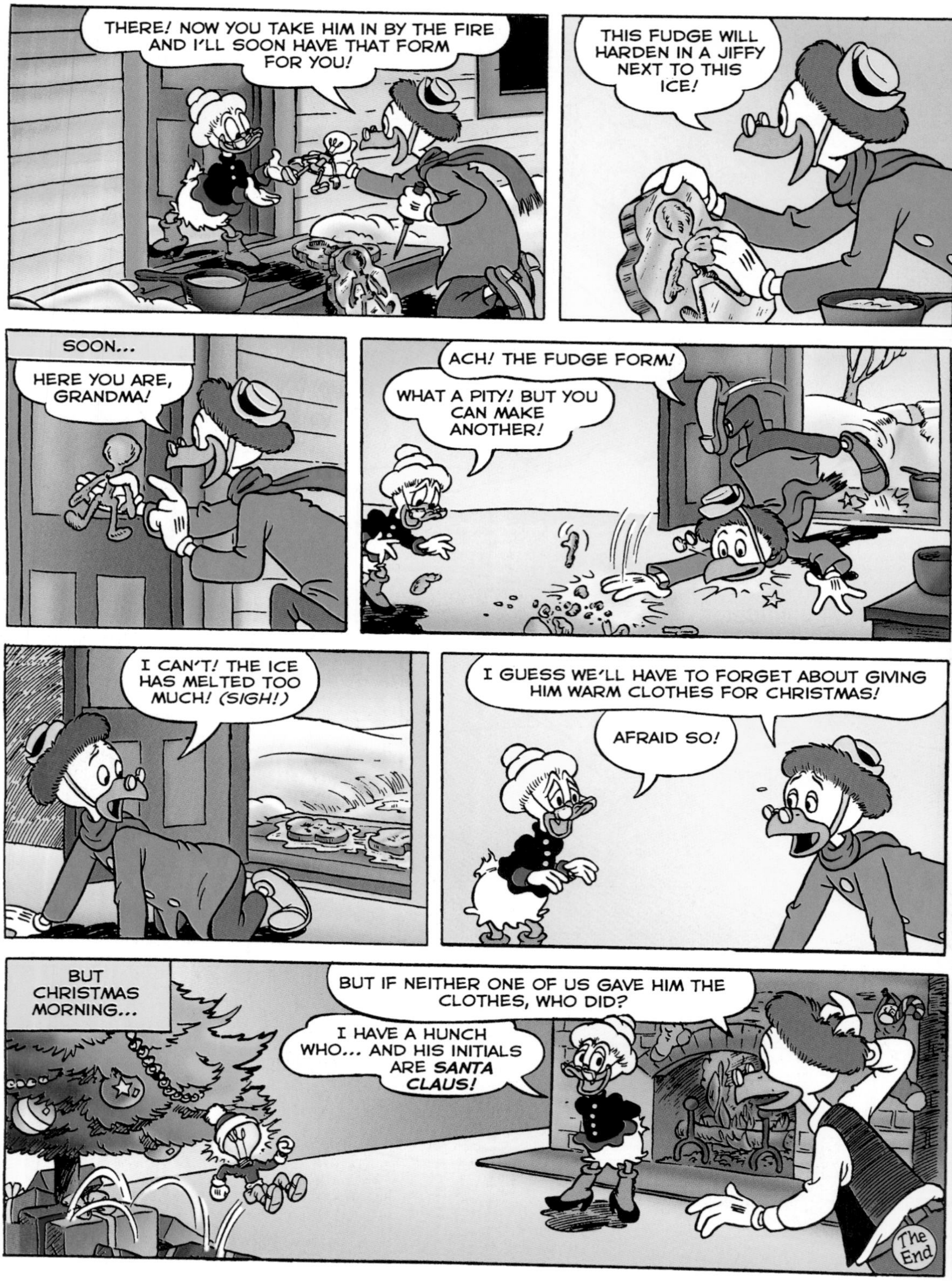
THERE! NOW YOU TAKE HIM IN BY THE FIRE AND I'LL SOON HAVE THAT FORM FOR YOU!
THIS FUDGE WILL HARDEN IN A JIFFY NEXT TO THIS ICE!
SOON...
HERE YOU ARE, GRANDMA!
ACH! THE FUDGE FORM!
WHAT A PITY! BUT YOU CAN MAKE ANOTHER!
I CAN'T! THE ICE HAS MELTED TOO MUCH! (SIGH!)
I GUESS WE'LL HAVE TO FORGET ABOUT GIVING HIM WARM CLOTHES FOR CHRISTMAS!
AFRAID SO!
BUT CHRISTMAS MORNING...
BUT IF NEITHER ONE OF US GAVE HIM THE CLOTHES, WHO DID?
I HAVE A HUNCH WHO... AND HIS INITIALS ARE SANTA CLAUS!
The End

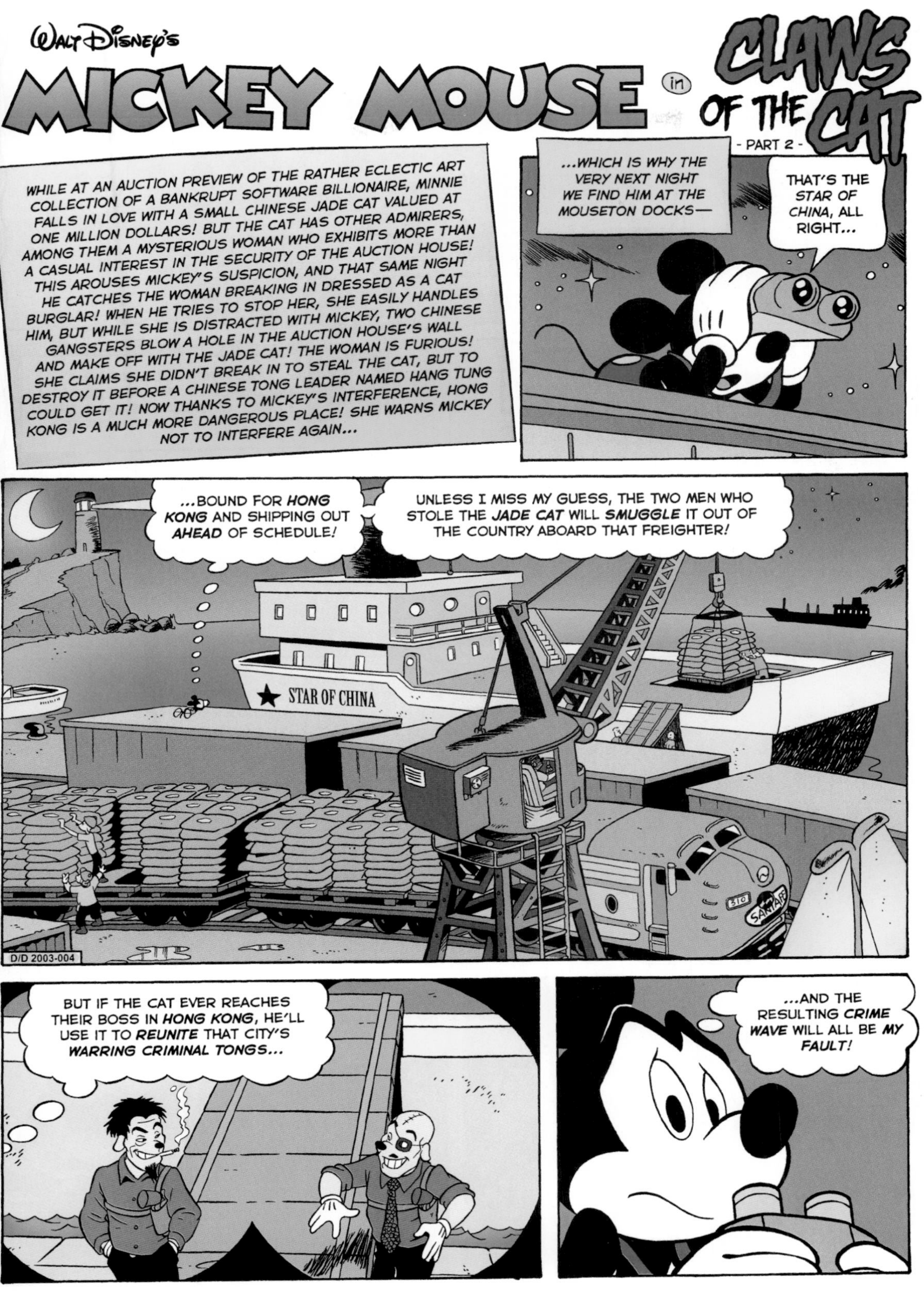
WALT DISNEY'S
MICKEY MOUSE in CLAWS OF THE CAT
- PART 2 -
WHILE AT AN AUCTION PREVIEW OF THE RATHER ECLECTIC ART COLLECTION OF A BANKRUPT SOFTWARE BILLIONAIRE, MINNIE FALLS IN LOVE WITH A SMALL CHINESE JADE CAT VALUED AT ONE MILLION DOLLARS! BUT THE CAT HAS OTHER ADMIRERS, AMONG THEM A MYSTERIOUS WOMAN WHO EXHIBITS MORE THAN A CASUAL INTEREST IN THE SECURITY OF THE AUCTION HOUSE! THIS AROUSES MICKEY'S SUSPICION, AND THAT SAME NIGHT HE CATCHES THE WOMAN BREAKING IN DRESSED AS A CAT BURGLAR! WHEN HE TRIES TO STOP HER, SHE EASILY HANDLES HIM, BUT WHILE SHE IS DISTRACTED WITH MICKEY, TWO CHINESE GANGSTERS BLOW A HOLE IN THE AUCTION HOUSE'S WALL AND MAKE OFF WITH THE JADE CAT! THE WOMAN IS FURIOUS! SHE CLAIMS SHE DIDN'T BREAK IN TO STEAL THE CAT, BUT TO DESTROY IT BEFORE A CHINESE TONG LEADER NAMED HANG TUNG COULD GET IT! NOW THANKS TO MICKEY'S INTERFERENCE, HONG KONG IS A MUCH MORE DANGEROUS PLACE! SHE WARNS MICKEY NOT TO INTERFERE AGAIN...
...WHICH IS WHY THE VERY NEXT NIGHT WE FIND HIM AT THE MOUSETON DOCKS—
THAT'S THE STAR OF CHINA, ALL RIGHT...
...BOUND FOR HONG KONG AND SHIPPING OUT AHEAD OF SCHEDULE!
UNLESS I MISS MY GUESS, THE TWO MEN WHO STOLE THE JADE CAT WILL SMUGGLE IT OUT OF THE COUNTRY ABOARD THAT FREIGHTER!
STAR OF CHINA
310
SANTA FE
D/D 2003-004
BUT IF THE CAT EVER REACHES THEIR BOSS IN HONG KONG, HE'LL USE IT TO REUNITE THAT CITY'S WARRING CRIMINAL TONGS...
...AND THE RESULTING CRIME WAVE WILL ALL BE MY FAULT!

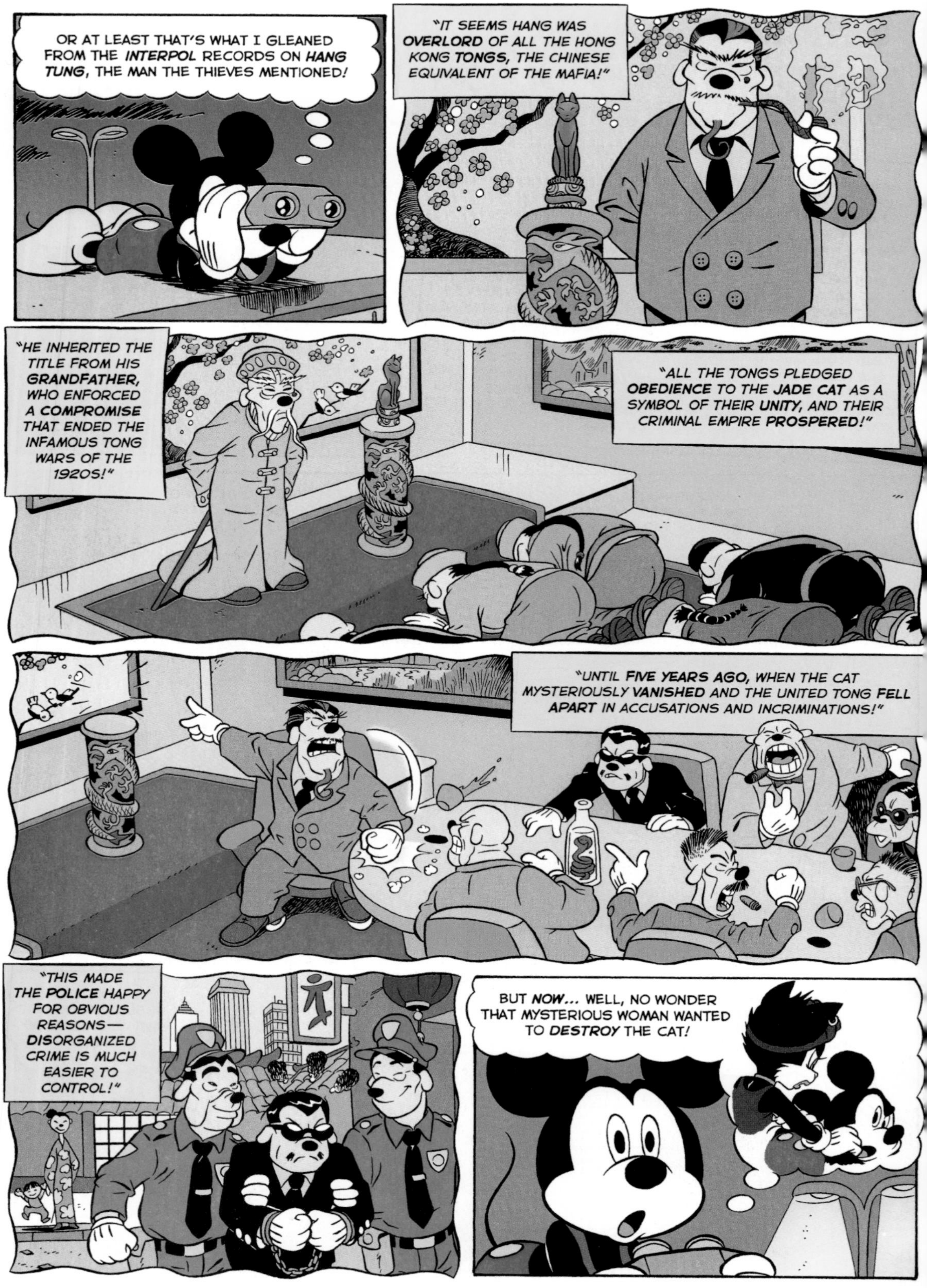
OR AT LEAST THAT'S WHAT I GLEANED FROM THE INTERPOL RECORDS ON HANG TUNG, THE MAN THE THIEVES MENTIONED!
"IT SEEMS HANG WAS OVERLORD OF ALL THE HONG KONG TONGS, THE CHINESE EQUIVALENT OF THE MAFIA!"
"HE INHERITED THE TITLE FROM HIS GRANDFATHER, WHO ENFORCED A COMPROMISE THAT ENDED THE INFAMOUS TONG WARS OF THE 1920S!"
"ALL THE TONGS PLEDGED OBEDIENCE TO THE JADE CAT AS A SYMBOL OF THEIR UNITY, AND THEIR CRIMINAL EMPIRE PROSPERED!"
"UNTIL FIVE YEARS AGO, WHEN THE CAT MYSTERIOUSLY VANISHED AND THE UNITED TONG FELL APART IN ACCUSATIONS AND INCRIMINATIONS!"
"THIS MADE THE POLICE HAPPY FOR OBVIOUS REASONS— DISORGANIZED CRIME IS MUCH EASIER TO CONTROL!"
BUT NOW... WELL, NO WONDER THAT MYSTERIOUS WOMAN WANTED TO DESTROY THE CAT!

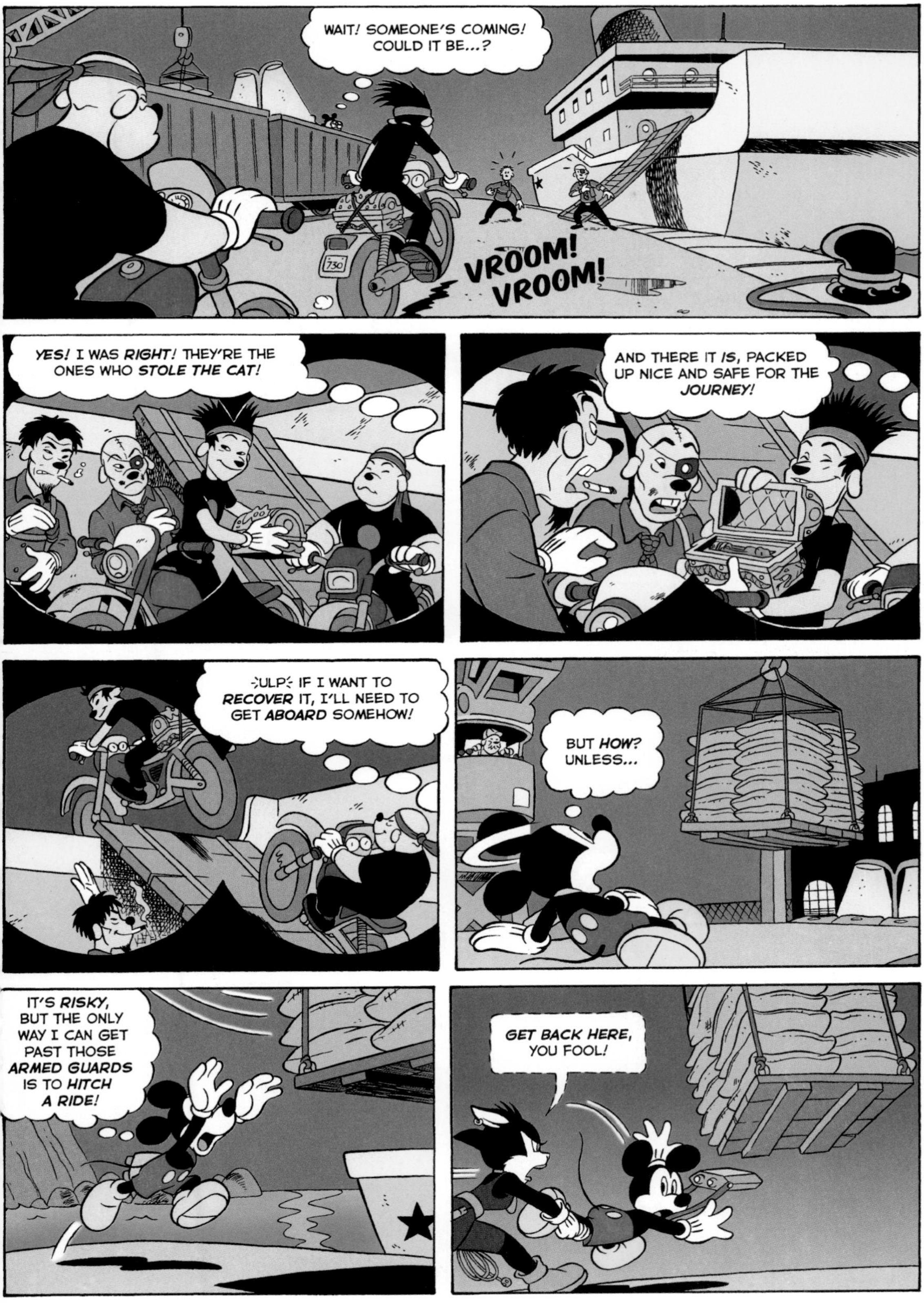
WAIT! SOMEONE'S COMING! COULD IT BE...?
VROOM! VROOM!
YES! I WAS RIGHT! THEY'RE THE ONES WHO STOLE THE CAT!
AND THERE IT IS, PACKED UP NICE AND SAFE FOR THE JOURNEY!
ULP IF I WANT TO RECOVER IT, I'LL NEED TO GET ABOARD SOMEHOW!
BUT HOW? UNLESS...
IT'S RISKY, BUT THE ONLY WAY I CAN GET PAST THOSE ARMED GUARDS IS TO HITCH A RIDE!
GET BACK HERE, YOU FOOL!

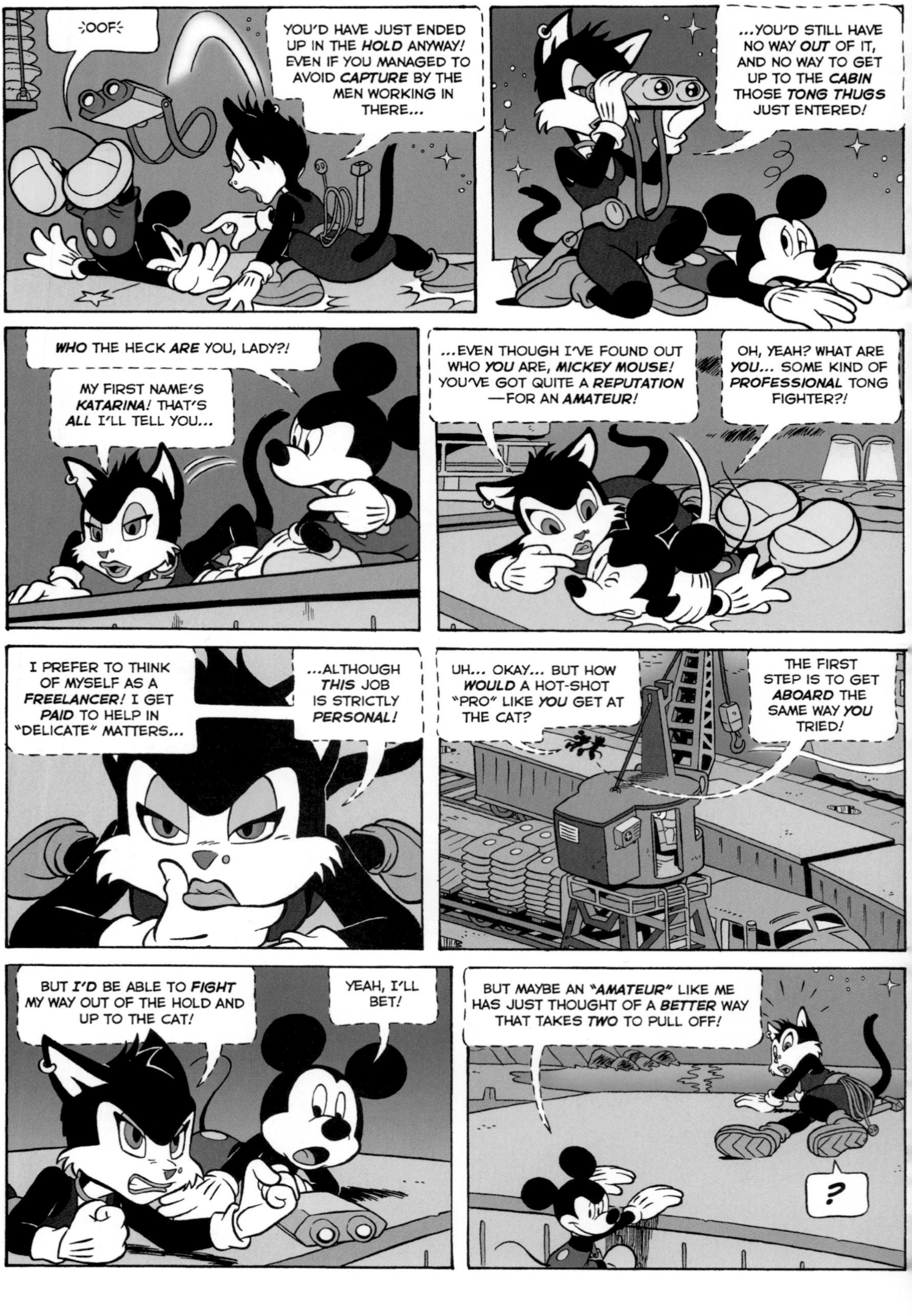
OOF
YOU'D HAVE JUST ENDED UP IN THE *HOLD* ANYWAY! EVEN IF YOU MANAGED TO AVOID *CAPTURE* BY THE MEN WORKING IN THERE...
...YOU'D STILL HAVE NO WAY *OUT* OF IT, AND NO WAY TO GET UP TO THE *CABIN* THOSE *TONG THUGS* JUST ENTERED!
WHO THE HECK *ARE* YOU, LADY?!
MY FIRST NAME'S *KATARINA!* THAT'S *ALL* I'LL TELL YOU...
...EVEN THOUGH I'VE FOUND OUT WHO *YOU* ARE, *MICKEY MOUSE!* YOU'VE GOT QUITE A *REPUTATION* —FOR AN *AMATEUR!*
OH, YEAH? WHAT ARE *YOU...* SOME KIND OF *PROFESSIONAL* TONG FIGHTER?!
I PREFER TO THINK OF MYSELF AS A *FREELANCER!* I GET *PAID* TO HELP IN "DELICATE" MATTERS...
...ALTHOUGH *THIS* JOB IS STRICTLY *PERSONAL!*
UH... OKAY... BUT HOW *WOULD* A HOT-SHOT "PRO" LIKE *YOU* GET AT THE CAT?
THE FIRST STEP IS TO GET *ABOARD* THE SAME WAY *YOU* TRIED!
BUT *I'D* BE ABLE TO *FIGHT* MY WAY OUT OF THE HOLD AND UP TO THE CAT!
YEAH, I'LL BET!
BUT MAYBE AN "*AMATEUR*" LIKE ME HAS JUST THOUGHT OF A *BETTER* WAY THAT TAKES *TWO* TO PULL OFF!
?

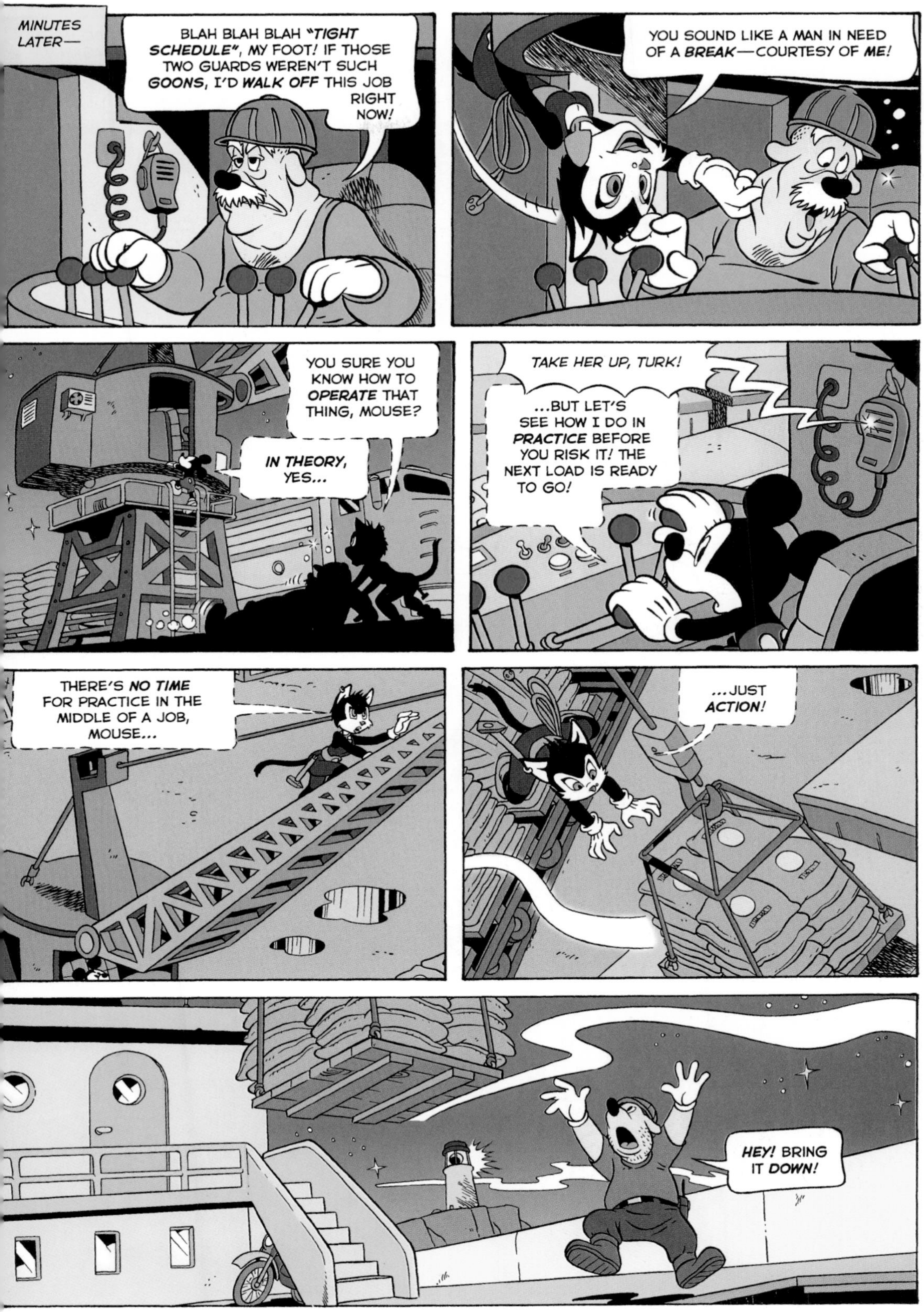
MINUTES LATER—
BLAH BLAH BLAH "TIGHT SCHEDULE", MY FOOT! IF THOSE TWO GUARDS WEREN'T SUCH GOONS, I'D WALK OFF THIS JOB RIGHT NOW!
YOU SOUND LIKE A MAN IN NEED OF A BREAK—COURTESY OF ME!
YOU SURE YOU KNOW HOW TO OPERATE THAT THING, MOUSE?
IN THEORY, YES...
TAKE HER UP, TURK!
...BUT LET'S SEE HOW I DO IN PRACTICE BEFORE YOU RISK IT! THE NEXT LOAD IS READY TO GO!
THERE'S NO TIME FOR PRACTICE IN THE MIDDLE OF A JOB, MOUSE...
...JUST ACTION!
HEY! BRING IT DOWN!

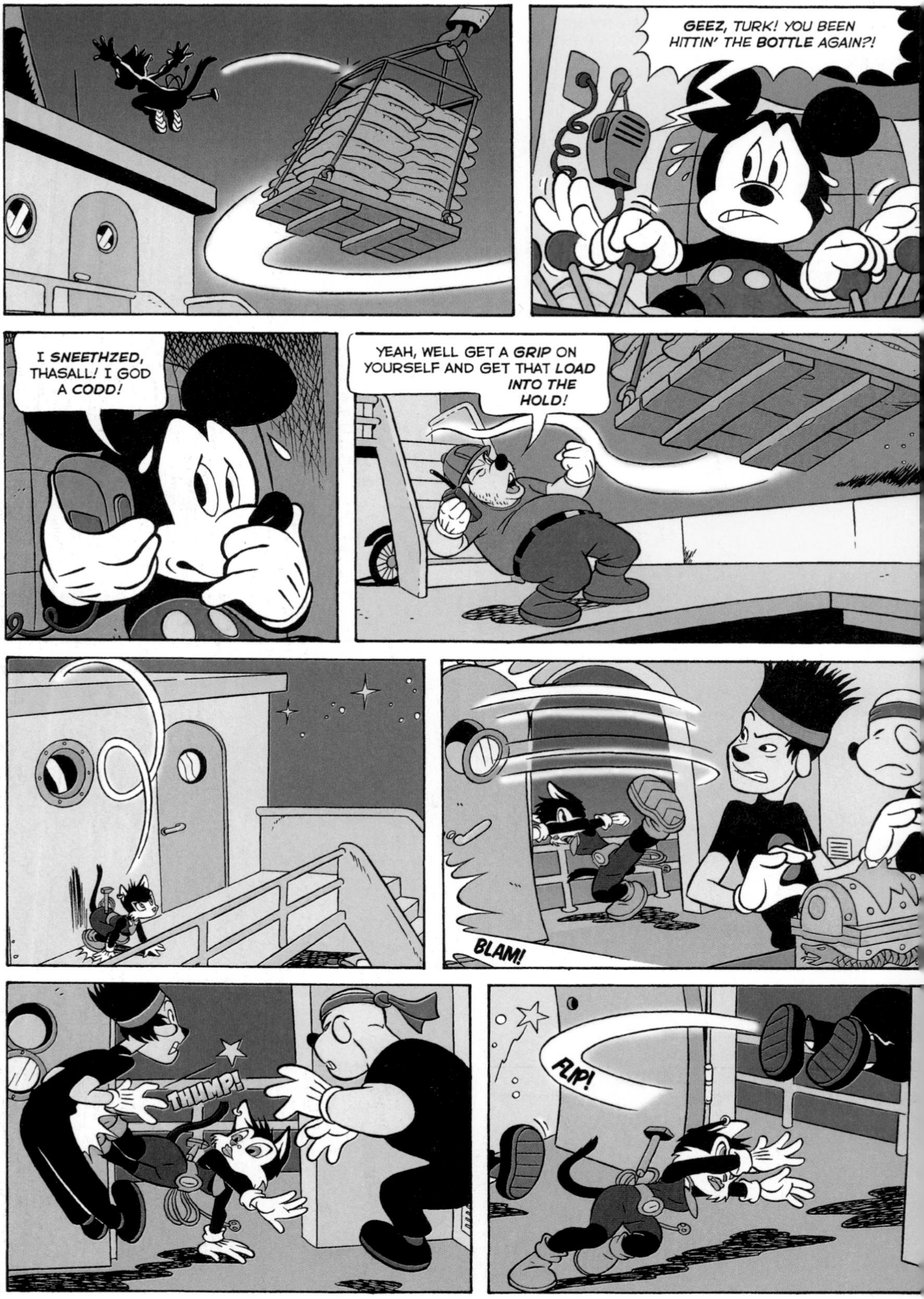
GEEZ, TURK! YOU BEEN HITTIN' THE BOTTLE AGAIN?!
I SNEETHZED, THASALL! I GOD A CODD!
YEAH, WELL GET A GRIP ON YOURSELF AND GET THAT LOAD INTO THE HOLD!
BLAM!
THUMP!
FLIP!

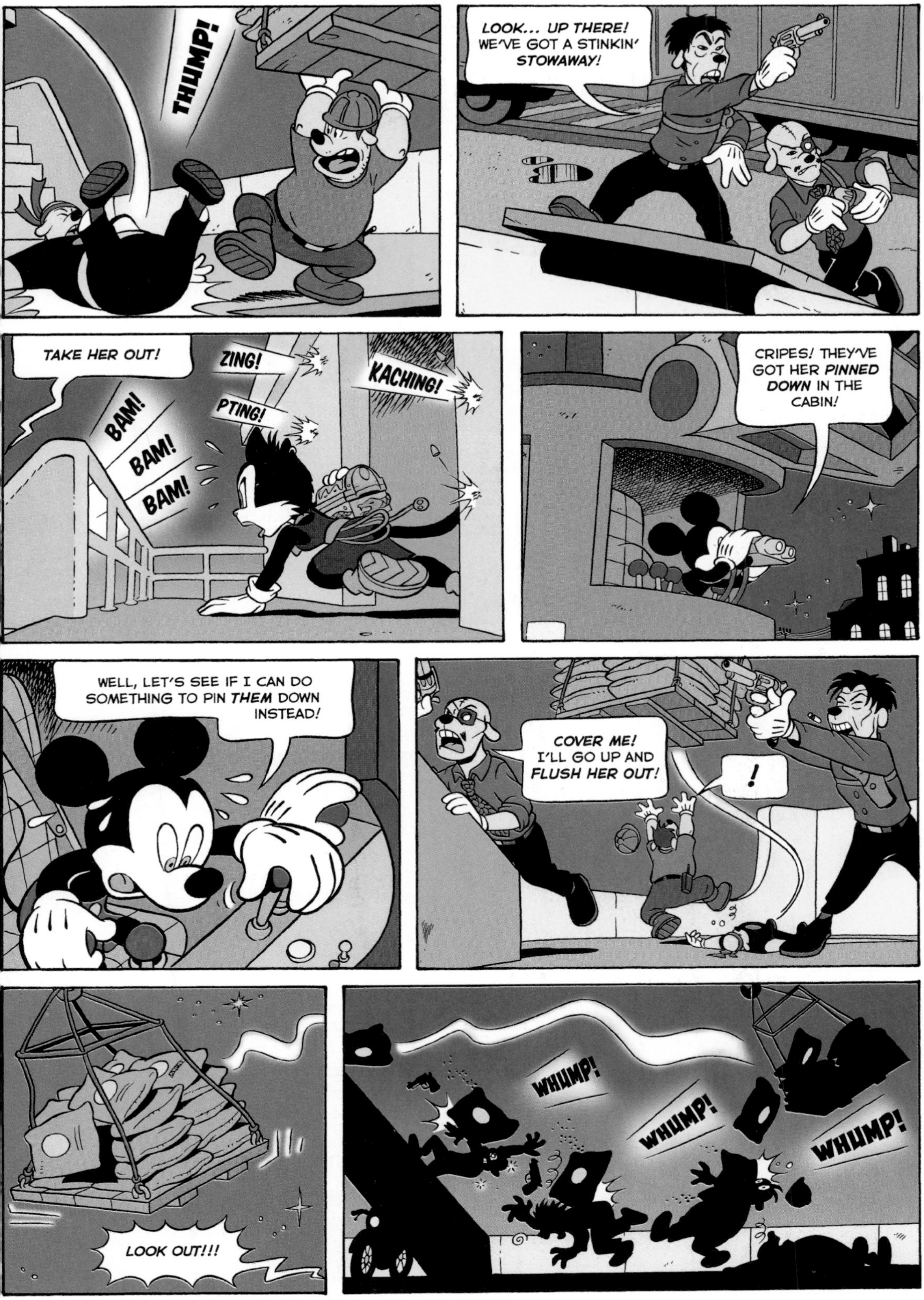
THUMP!
LOOK... UP THERE! WE'VE GOT A STINKIN' STOWAWAY!
TAKE HER OUT!
ZING!
KACHING!
BAM!
PTING!
BAM!
BAM!
CRIPES! THEY'VE GOT HER PINNED DOWN IN THE CABIN!
WELL, LET'S SEE IF I CAN DO SOMETHING TO PIN THEM DOWN INSTEAD!
COVER ME! I'LL GO UP AND FLUSH HER OUT!
!
LOOK OUT!!!
WHUMP!
WHUMP!
WHUMP!

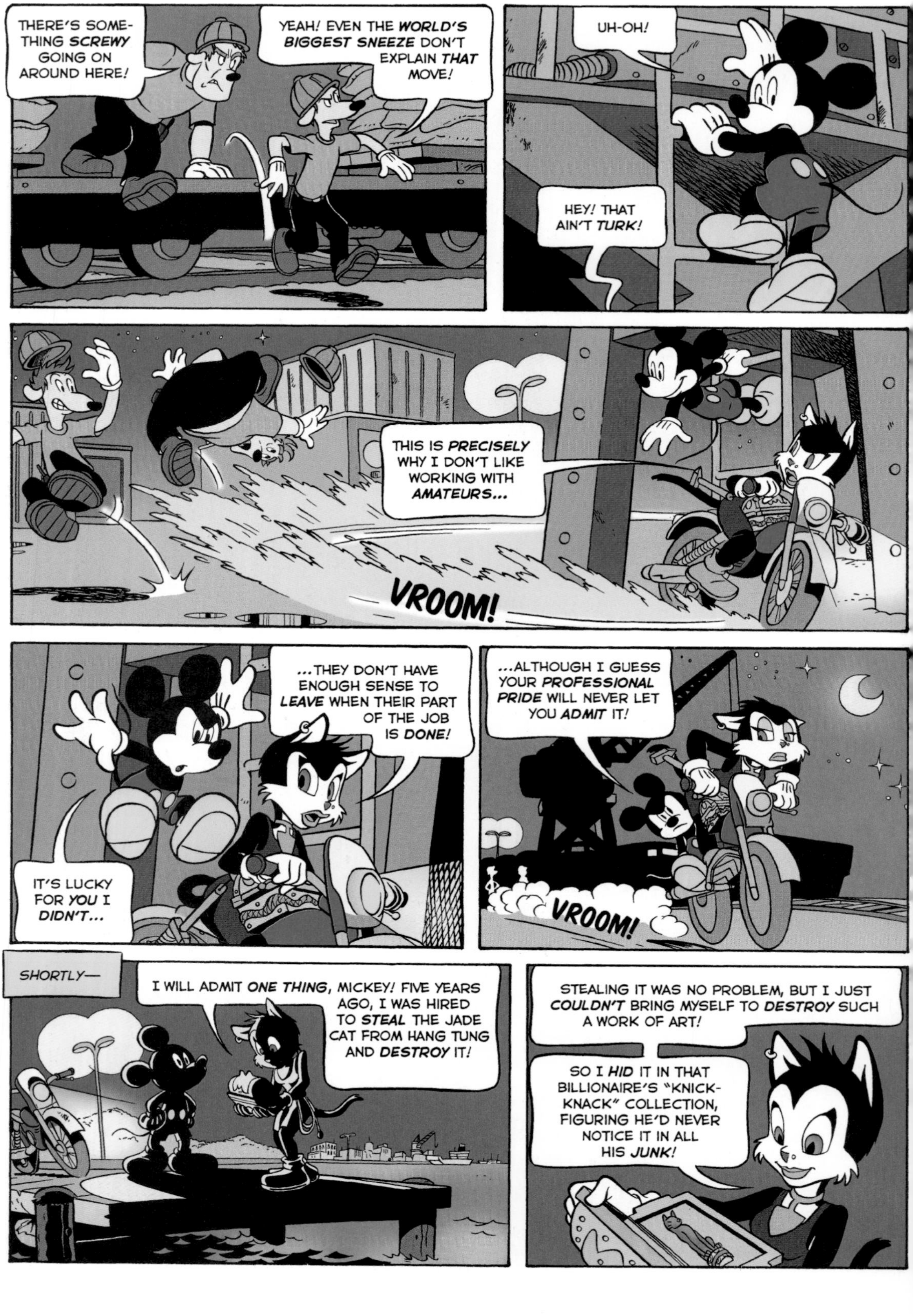

THERE'S SOMETHING SCREWY GOING ON AROUND HERE!
YEAH! EVEN THE WORLD'S BIGGEST SNEEZE DON'T EXPLAIN THAT MOVE!
UH-OH!
HEY! THAT AIN'T TURK!
THIS IS PRECISELY WHY I DON'T LIKE WORKING WITH AMATEURS...
VROOM!
...THEY DON'T HAVE ENOUGH SENSE TO LEAVE WHEN THEIR PART OF THE JOB IS DONE!
IT'S LUCKY FOR YOU I DIDN'T...
...ALTHOUGH I GUESS YOUR PROFESSIONAL PRIDE WILL NEVER LET YOU ADMIT IT!
VROOM!
SHORTLY—
I WILL ADMIT ONE THING, MICKEY! FIVE YEARS AGO, I WAS HIRED TO STEAL THE JADE CAT FROM HANG TUNG AND DESTROY IT!
STEALING IT WAS NO PROBLEM, BUT I JUST COULDN'T BRING MYSELF TO DESTROY SUCH A WORK OF ART!
SO I HID IT IN THAT BILLIONAIRE'S "KNICK-KNACK" COLLECTION, FIGURING HE'D NEVER NOTICE IT IN ALL HIS JUNK!

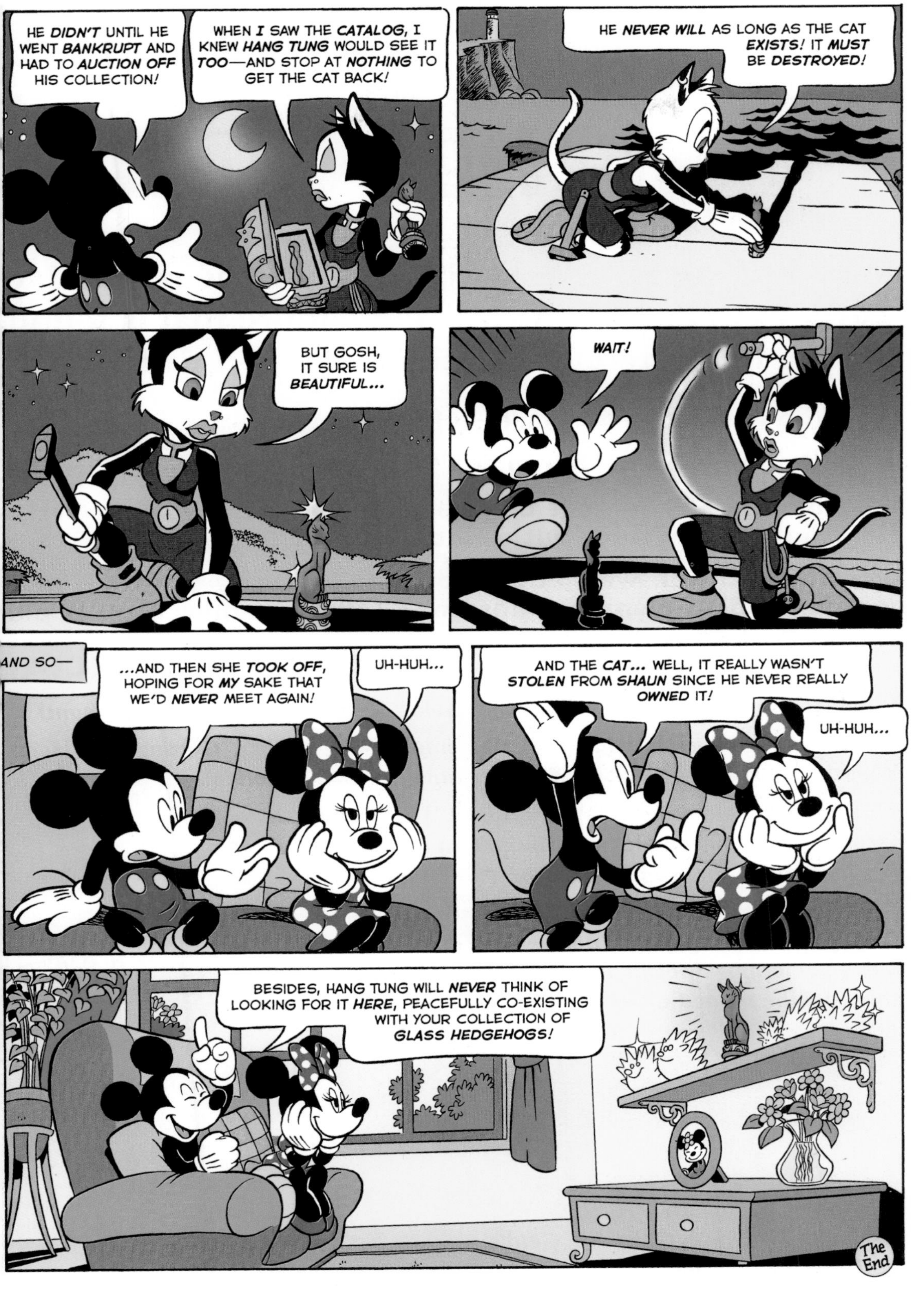
HE DIDN'T UNTIL HE WENT BANKRUPT AND HAD TO AUCTION OFF HIS COLLECTION!
WHEN I SAW THE CATALOG, I KNEW HANG TUNG WOULD SEE IT TOO—AND STOP AT NOTHING TO GET THE CAT BACK!
HE NEVER WILL AS LONG AS THE CAT EXISTS! IT MUST BE DESTROYED!
BUT GOSH, IT SURE IS BEAUTIFUL...
WAIT!
AND SO—
...AND THEN SHE TOOK OFF, HOPING FOR MY SAKE THAT WE'D NEVER MEET AGAIN!
UH-HUH...
AND THE CAT... WELL, IT REALLY WASN'T STOLEN FROM SHAUN SINCE HE NEVER REALLY OWNED IT!
UH-HUH...
BESIDES, HANG TUNG WILL NEVER THINK OF LOOKING FOR IT HERE, PEACEFULLY CO-EXISTING WITH YOUR COLLECTION OF GLASS HEDGEHOGS!
The End

DONALDIST POP QUIZ!

don • ald • ism \ dän'-ld-iz'-em \ *n* : the research o. Disney comics, and/or the fan culture that is found among Disney comics aficionados (Jon Gisle, 1973)

1. Who is Scrooge McDuck's "old flame" from the Yukon?

2. Who *wants* to be "Scroogie's" *new* love interest?

3. And how will Scrooge be celebrating his birthday this year? (Hint: *Not* by going out on a date!)

You can find the answers at the bottom of this page, but you'll hav more fun finding them in Gemstone's 160-page anniversary book:

UNCLE SCROOGE: A LITTLE SOMETHING SPECIAL

- *Discover Carl Barks' "Seven Cities of Cibola," Scrooge's richest treasure hunt!*

- *Watch Scrooge earn his Number One Dime in Tony Strobl's "Getting That Health Wealthy Feeling" — uncut for the first time in North America!*

- *Thrilling tightwad tales by Marco Rota ("The Money Ocean"), William Van Horn ("Windfall on Mt. G'zoontight"), and Romano Scarpa (the never-before-reprinted "Witness Persecution")!*

- *Don Rosa's feature-length anniversary epic "A Little Something Special"... what else could this book be named after?*

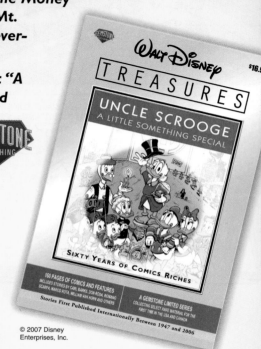

© 2007 Disney
Enterprises, Inc.

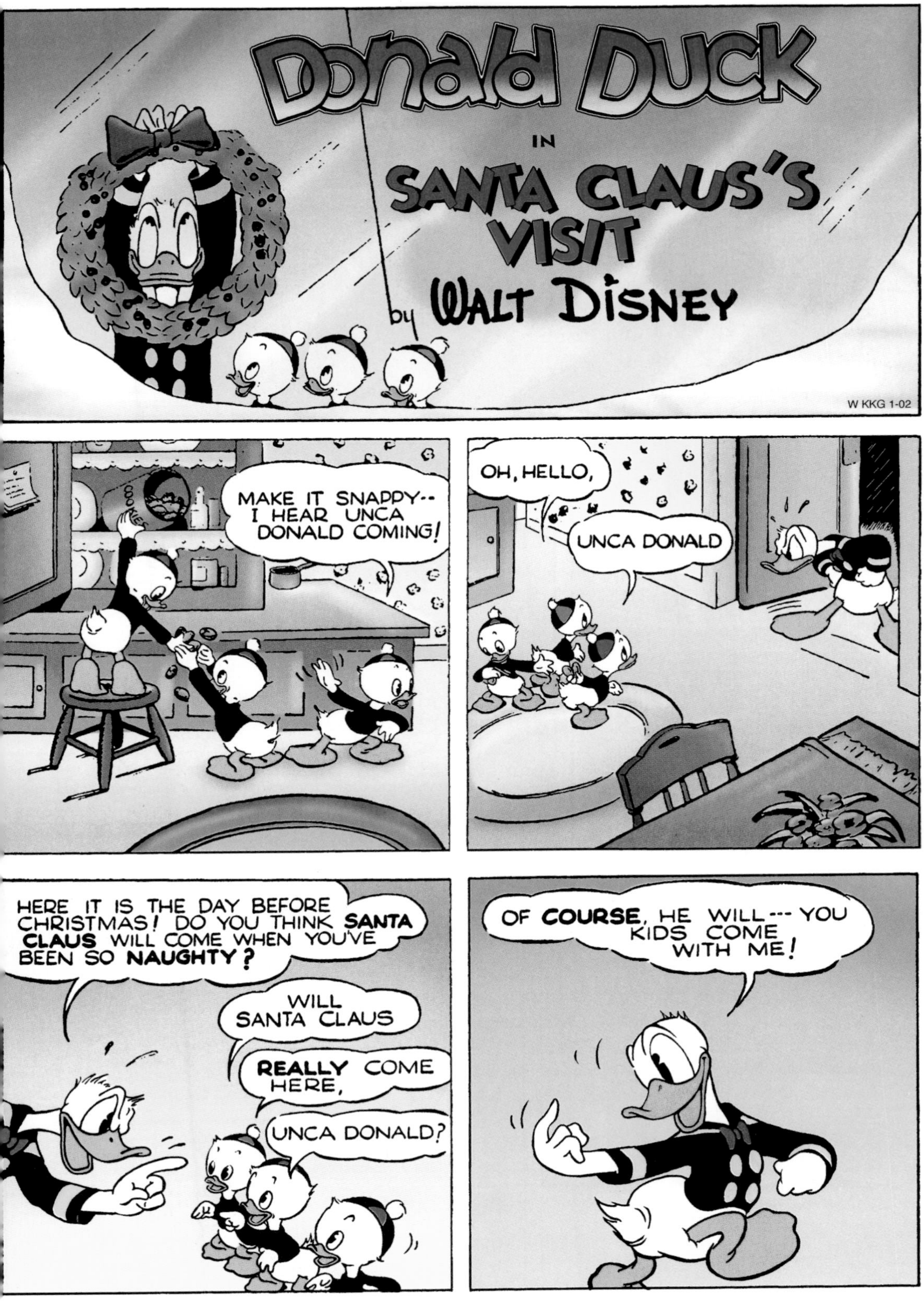

DONALD DUCK
IN
SANTA CLAUS'S VISIT
by WALT DISNEY
W KKG 1-02
COOKIES
MAKE IT SNAPPY-- I HEAR UNCA DONALD COMING!
OH, HELLO,
UNCA DONALD
HERE IT IS THE DAY BEFORE CHRISTMAS! DO YOU THINK **SANTA CLAUS** WILL COME WHEN YOU'VE BEEN SO **NAUGHTY**?
WILL SANTA CLAUS
REALLY COME HERE,
UNCA DONALD?
OF **COURSE**, HE WILL --- YOU KIDS COME WITH ME!

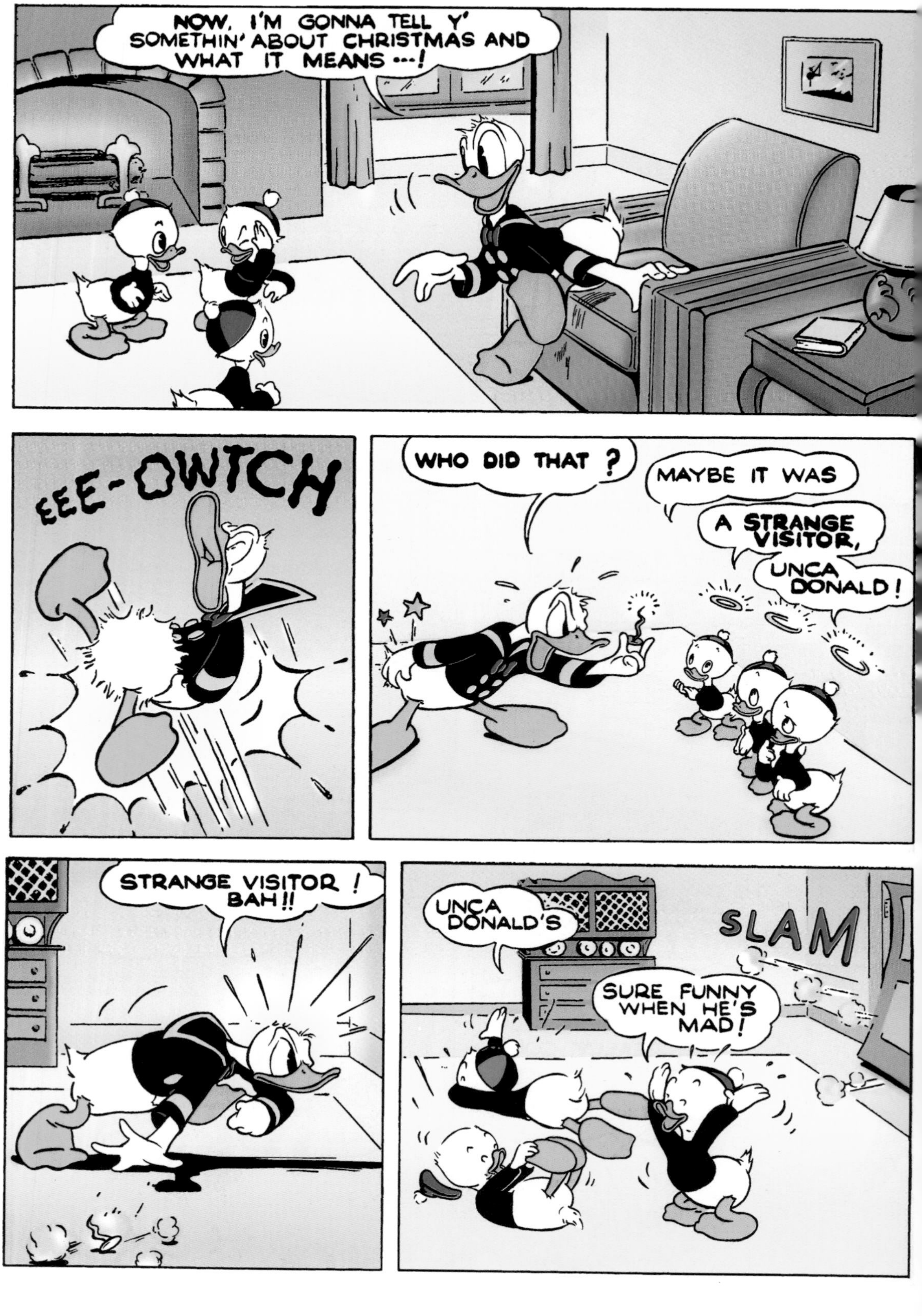
NOW, I'M GONNA TELL Y' SOMETHIN' ABOUT CHRISTMAS AND WHAT IT MEANS ---!
EEE-OWTCH
WHO DID THAT ?
MAYBE IT WAS
A STRANGE VISITOR,
UNCA DONALD!
STRANGE VISITOR ! BAH!!
UNCA DONALD'S
SLAM
SURE FUNNY WHEN HE'S MAD!

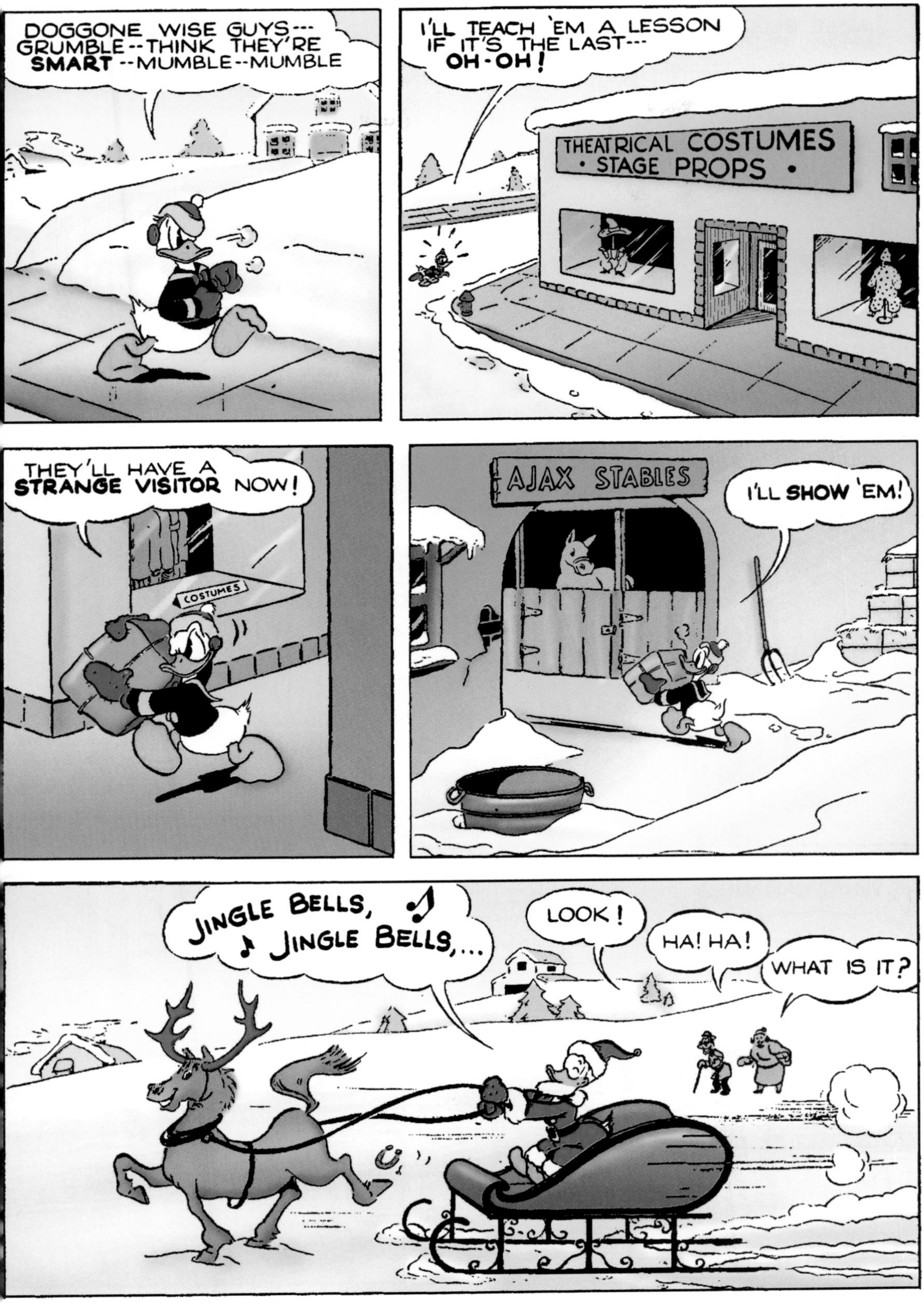
DOGGONE WISE GUYS--- GRUMBLE--THINK THEY'RE SMART --MUMBLE--MUMBLE
I'LL TEACH 'EM A LESSON IF IT'S THE LAST--- OH-OH!
THEATRICAL COSTUMES • STAGE PROPS •
THEY'LL HAVE A STRANGE VISITOR NOW!
COSTUMES
AJAX STABLES
I'LL SHOW 'EM!
JINGLE BELLS, JINGLE BELLS,...
LOOK!
HA! HA!
WHAT IS IT?

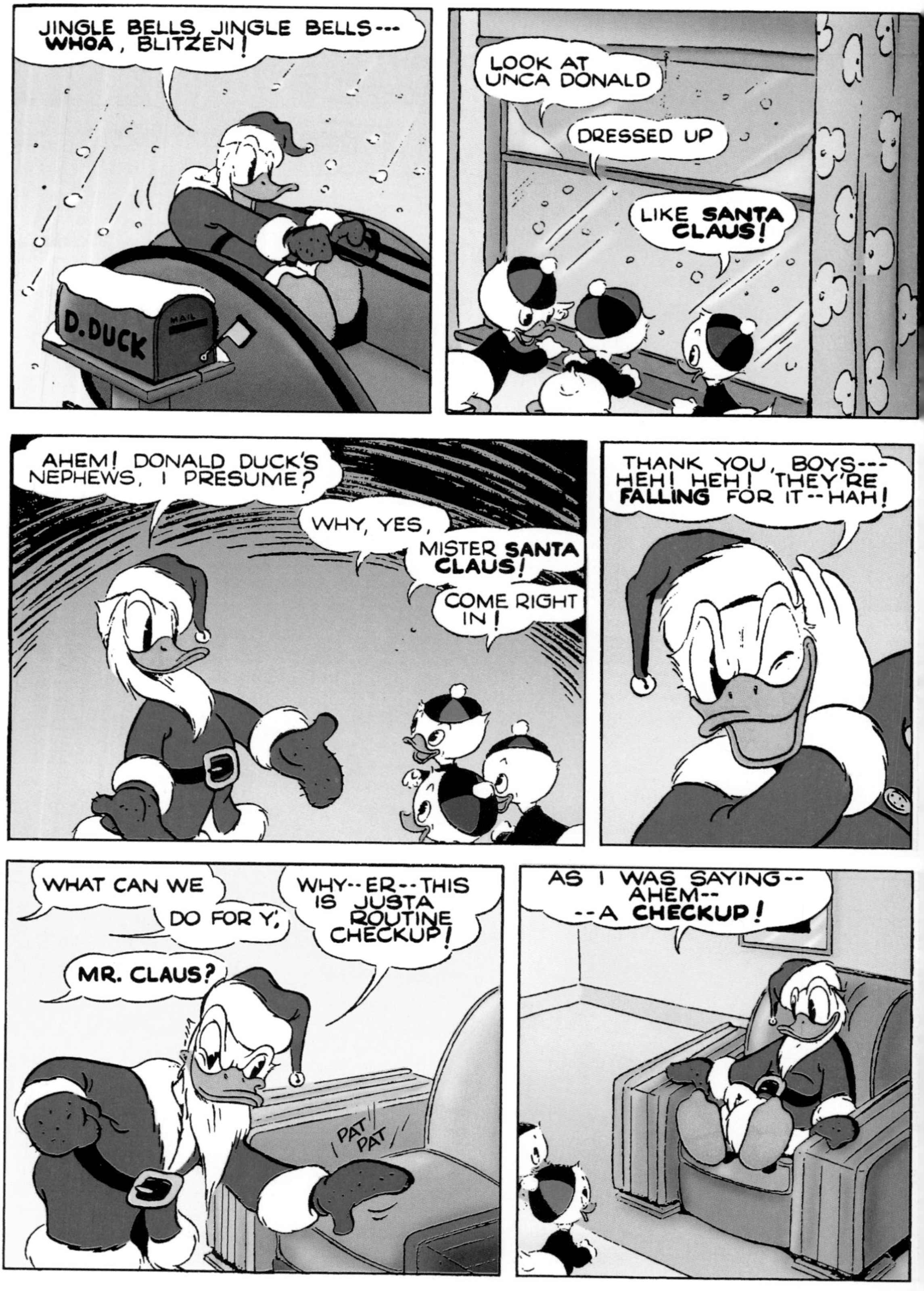
JINGLE BELLS, JINGLE BELLS--- **WHOA**, BLITZEN!
D. DUCK
MAIL
LOOK AT UNCA DONALD
DRESSED UP
LIKE **SANTA CLAUS**!
AHEM! DONALD DUCK'S NEPHEWS, I PRESUME?
WHY, YES,
MISTER **SANTA CLAUS**!
COME RIGHT IN!
THANK YOU, BOYS--- HEH! HEH! THEY'RE **FALLING** FOR IT--HAH!
WHAT CAN WE
DO FOR Y',
MR. CLAUS?
WHY--ER--THIS IS JUSTA ROUTINE CHECKUP!
PAT PAT
AS I WAS SAYING-- AHEM-- --A **CHECKUP**!

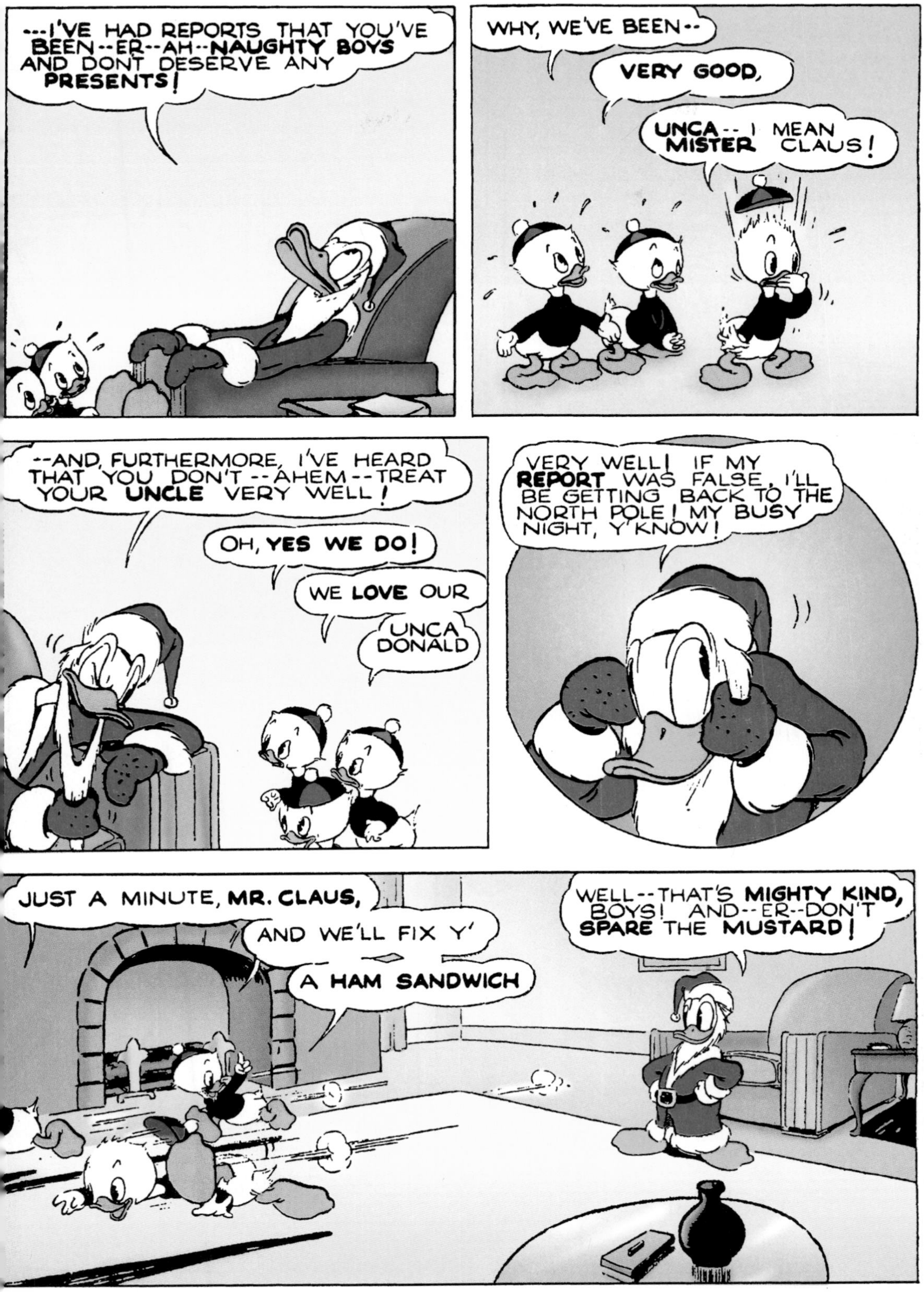
--I'VE HAD REPORTS THAT YOU'VE BEEN--ER--AH--NAUGHTY BOYS AND DON'T DESERVE ANY PRESENTS!
WHY, WE'VE BEEN--
VERY GOOD,
UNCA-- I MEAN MISTER CLAUS!
--AND, FURTHERMORE, I'VE HEARD THAT YOU DON'T--AHEM--TREAT YOUR UNCLE VERY WELL!
OH, YES WE DO!
WE LOVE OUR
UNCA DONALD
VERY WELL! IF MY REPORT WAS FALSE, I'LL BE GETTING BACK TO THE NORTH POLE! MY BUSY NIGHT, Y'KNOW!
JUST A MINUTE, MR. CLAUS,
AND WE'LL FIX Y'
A HAM SANDWICH
WELL--THAT'S MIGHTY KIND, BOYS! AND--ER--DON'T SPARE THE MUSTARD!

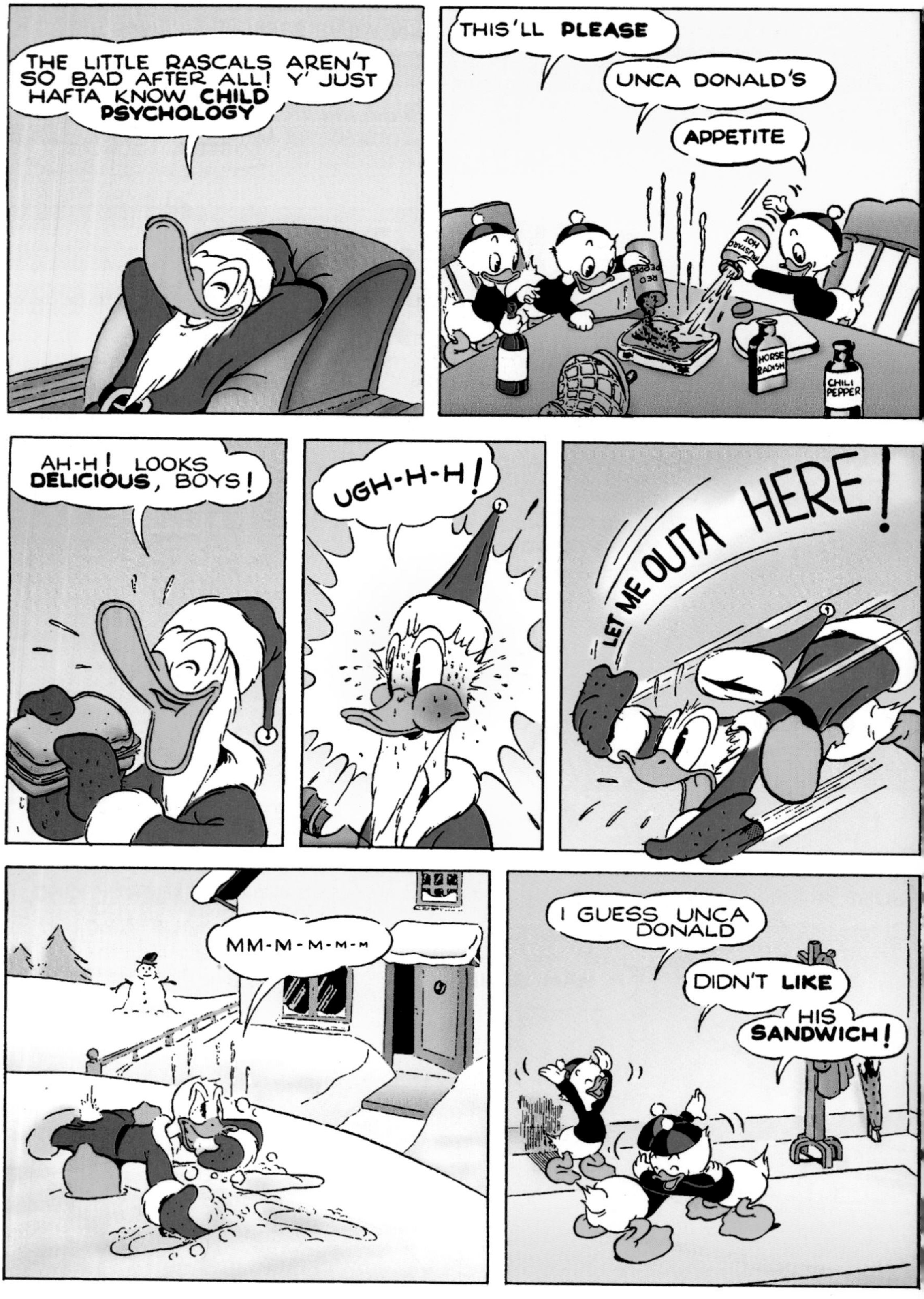
THE LITTLE RASCALS AREN'T SO BAD AFTER ALL! Y' JUST HAFTA KNOW **CHILD PSYCHOLOGY**
THIS'LL **PLEASE**
UNCA DONALD'S
APPETITE
RED PEPPER
HOT MUSTARD
HORSE RADISH
CHILI PEPPER
AH-H! LOOKS **DELICIOUS**, BOYS!
UGH-H-H!
LET ME OUTA HERE!
MM-M-M-M-M
I GUESS UNCA DONALD
DIDN'T **LIKE**
HIS **SANDWICH**!

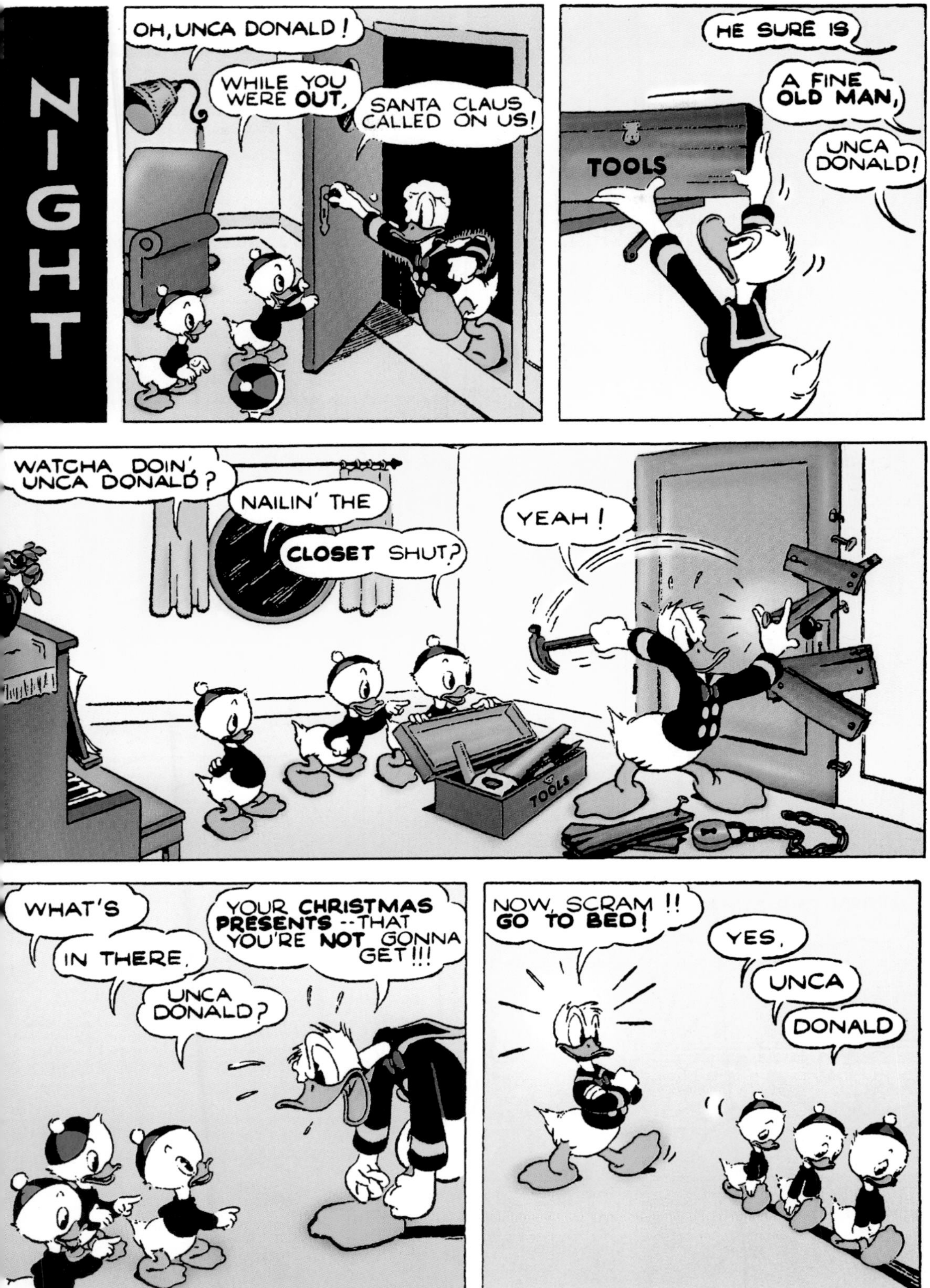
NIGHT
OH, UNCA DONALD!
WHILE YOU WERE OUT,
SANTA CLAUS CALLED ON US!
HE SURE IS
A FINE OLD MAN,
UNCA DONALD!
TOOLS
WATCHA DOIN', UNCA DONALD?
NAILIN' THE
CLOSET SHUT?
YEAH!
TOOLS
WHAT'S
IN THERE,
UNCA DONALD?
YOUR CHRISTMAS PRESENTS --THAT YOU'RE NOT GONNA GET!!!
NOW, SCRAM!! GO TO BED!
YES,
UNCA
DONALD

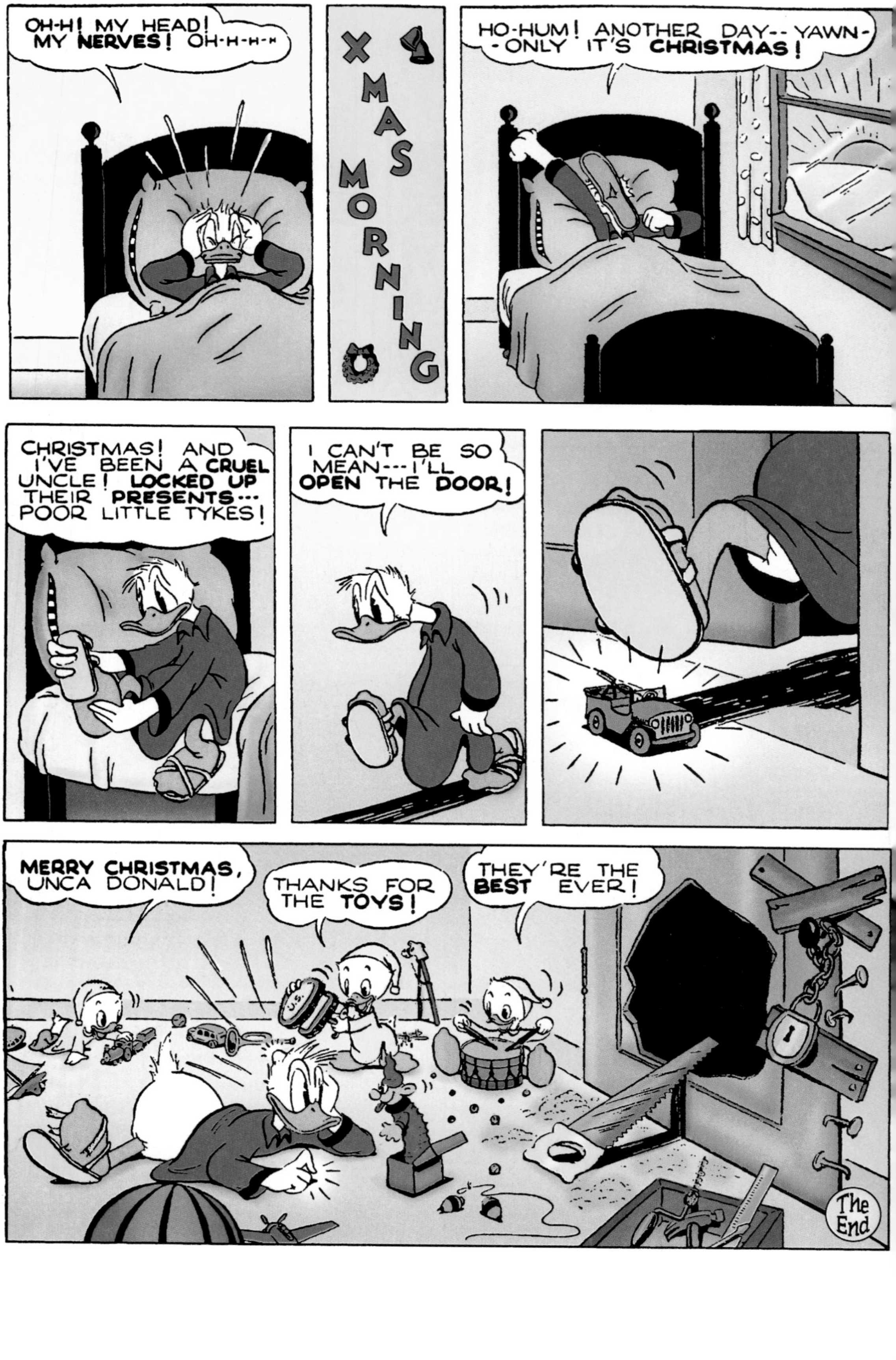
OH-H! MY HEAD! MY NERVES! OH-H-H-H
XMAS MORNING
HO-HUM! ANOTHER DAY-- YAWN- -ONLY IT'S CHRISTMAS!
CHRISTMAS! AND I'VE BEEN A CRUEL UNCLE! LOCKED UP THEIR PRESENTS--- POOR LITTLE TYKES!
I CAN'T BE SO MEAN---I'LL OPEN THE DOOR!
MERRY CHRISTMAS, UNCA DONALD!
THANKS FOR THE TOYS!
THEY'RE THE BEST EVER!
The End

Walt Disney's GOOFY in PUTTING IT ALL TOGETHER

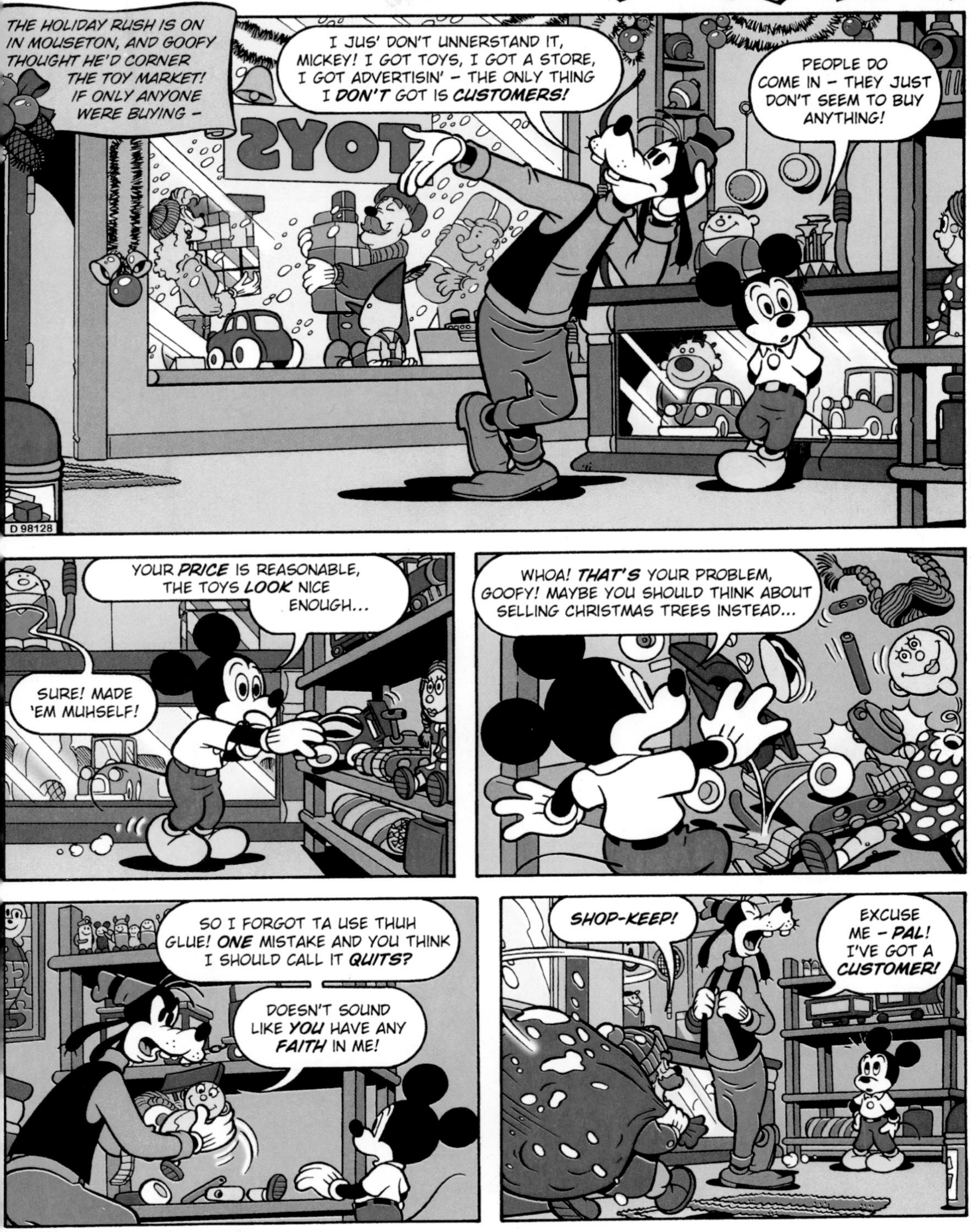
THE HOLIDAY RUSH IS ON IN MOUSETON, AND GOOFY THOUGHT HE'D CORNER THE TOY MARKET! IF ONLY ANYONE WERE BUYING –
TOYS
I JUS' DON'T UNNERSTAND IT, MICKEY! I GOT TOYS, I GOT A STORE, I GOT ADVERTISIN' – THE ONLY THING I DON'T GOT IS CUSTOMERS!
PEOPLE DO COME IN – THEY JUST DON'T SEEM TO BUY ANYTHING!
D 98128
YOUR PRICE IS REASONABLE, THE TOYS LOOK NICE ENOUGH...
SURE! MADE 'EM MUHSELF!
WHOA! THAT'S YOUR PROBLEM, GOOFY! MAYBE YOU SHOULD THINK ABOUT SELLING CHRISTMAS TREES INSTEAD...
SO I FORGOT TA USE THUH GLUE! ONE MISTAKE AND YOU THINK I SHOULD CALL IT QUITS?
DOESN'T SOUND LIKE YOU HAVE ANY FAITH IN ME!
SHOP-KEEP!
EXCUSE ME – PAL! I'VE GOT A CUSTOMER!

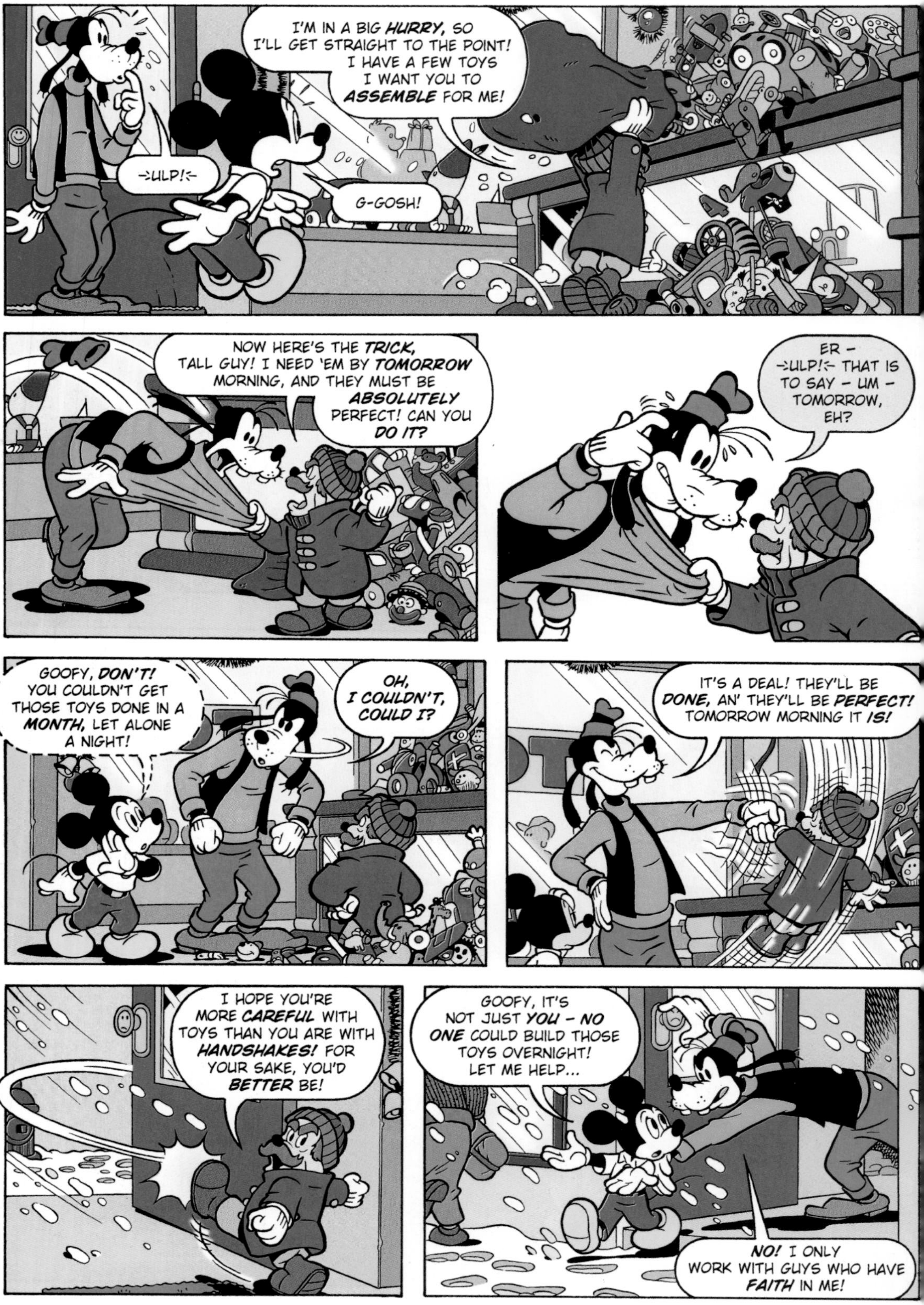
I'M IN A BIG HURRY, SO I'LL GET STRAIGHT TO THE POINT! I HAVE A FEW TOYS I WANT YOU TO ASSEMBLE FOR ME!
-ULP!-
G-GOSH!
NOW HERE'S THE TRICK, TALL GUY! I NEED 'EM BY TOMORROW MORNING, AND THEY MUST BE ABSOLUTELY PERFECT! CAN YOU DO IT?
ER – -ULP!- THAT IS TO SAY – UM – TOMORROW, EH?
GOOFY, DON'T! YOU COULDN'T GET THOSE TOYS DONE IN A MONTH, LET ALONE A NIGHT!
OH, I COULDN'T, COULD I?
IT'S A DEAL! THEY'LL BE DONE, AN' THEY'LL BE PERFECT! TOMORROW MORNING IT IS!
I HOPE YOU'RE MORE CAREFUL WITH TOYS THAN YOU ARE WITH HANDSHAKES! FOR YOUR SAKE, YOU'D BETTER BE!
GOOFY, IT'S NOT JUST YOU – NO ONE COULD BUILD THOSE TOYS OVERNIGHT! LET ME HELP...
NO! I ONLY WORK WITH GUYS WHO HAVE FAITH IN ME!

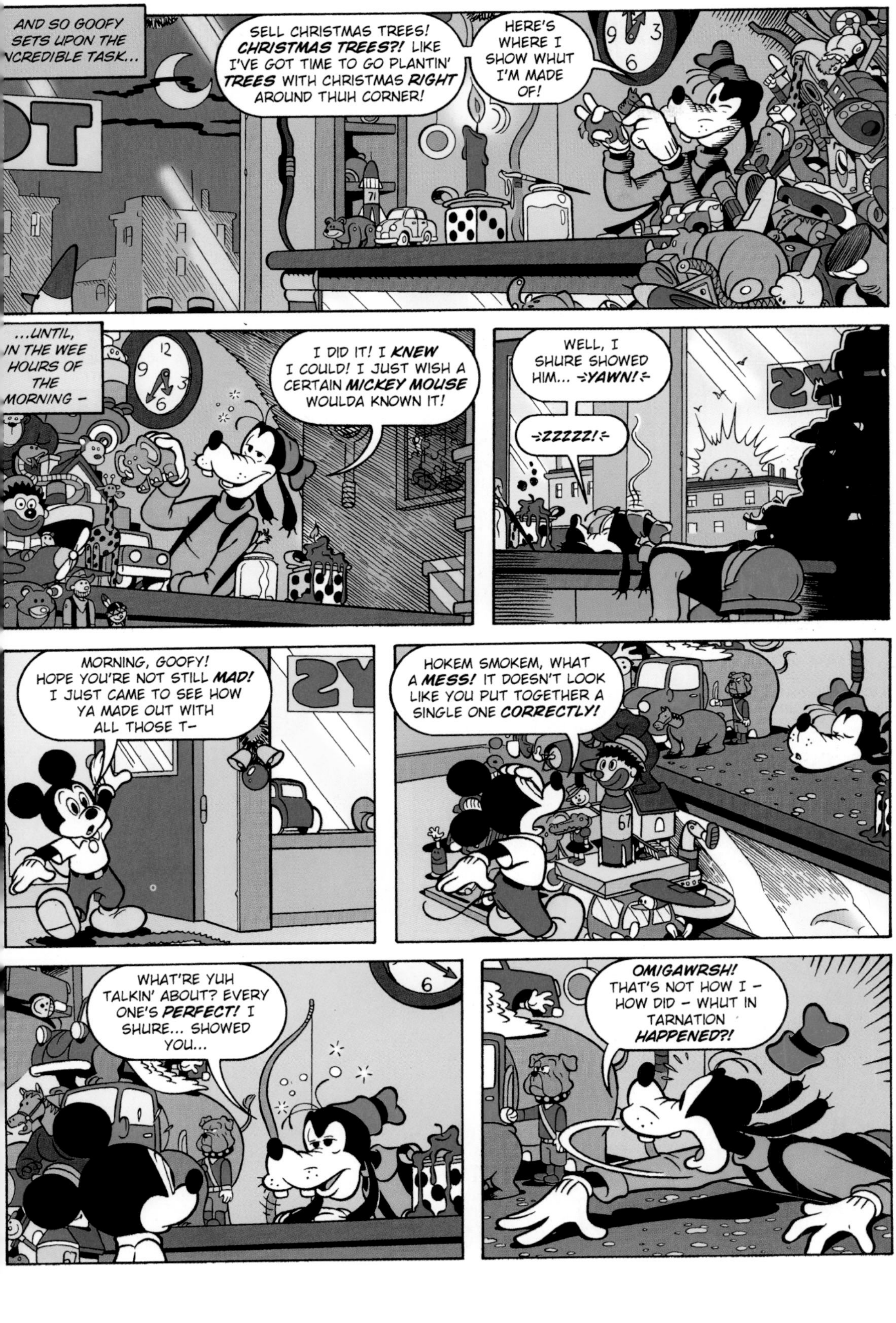

AND SO GOOFY SETS UPON THE INCREDIBLE TASK...
SELL CHRISTMAS TREES! CHRISTMAS TREES?! LIKE I'VE GOT TIME TO GO PLANTIN' TREES WITH CHRISTMAS RIGHT AROUND THUH CORNER!
HERE'S WHERE I SHOW WHUT I'M MADE OF!
...UNTIL, IN THE WEE HOURS OF THE MORNING –
I DID IT! I KNEW I COULD! I JUST WISH A CERTAIN MICKEY MOUSE WOULDA KNOWN IT!
WELL, I SHURE SHOWED HIM... YAWN!
ZZZZZ!
MORNING, GOOFY! HOPE YOU'RE NOT STILL MAD! I JUST CAME TO SEE HOW YA MADE OUT WITH ALL THOSE T–
HOKEM SMOKEM, WHAT A MESS! IT DOESN'T LOOK LIKE YOU PUT TOGETHER A SINGLE ONE CORRECTLY!
WHAT'RE YUH TALKIN' ABOUT? EVERY ONE'S PERFECT! I SHURE... SHOWED YOU...
OMIGAWRSH! THAT'S NOT HOW I – HOW DID – WHUT IN TARNATION HAPPENED?!

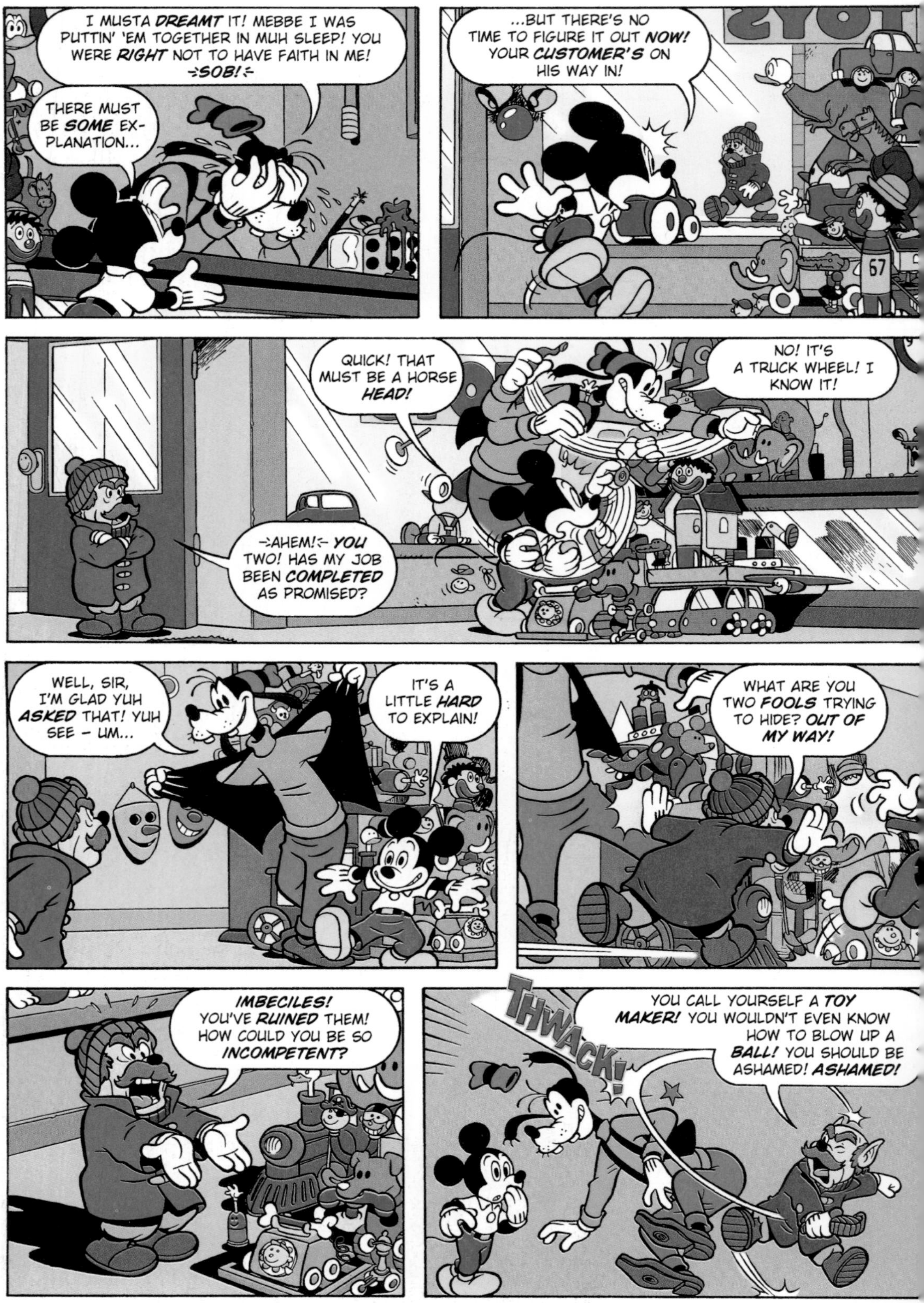
I MUSTA DREAMT IT! MEBBE I WAS PUTTIN' 'EM TOGETHER IN MUH SLEEP! YOU WERE RIGHT NOT TO HAVE FAITH IN ME! SOB!
THERE MUST BE SOME EX-PLANATION...
...BUT THERE'S NO TIME TO FIGURE IT OUT NOW! YOUR CUSTOMER'S ON HIS WAY IN!
QUICK! THAT MUST BE A HORSE HEAD!
NO! IT'S A TRUCK WHEEL! I KNOW IT!
AHEM! YOU TWO! HAS MY JOB BEEN COMPLETED AS PROMISED?
WELL, SIR, I'M GLAD YUH ASKED THAT! YUH SEE – UM...
IT'S A LITTLE HARD TO EXPLAIN!
WHAT ARE YOU TWO FOOLS TRYING TO HIDE? OUT OF MY WAY!
IMBECILES! YOU'VE RUINED THEM! HOW COULD YOU BE SO INCOMPETENT?
THWACK!
YOU CALL YOURSELF A TOY MAKER! YOU WOULDN'T EVEN KNOW HOW TO BLOW UP A BALL! YOU SHOULD BE ASHAMED! ASHAMED!

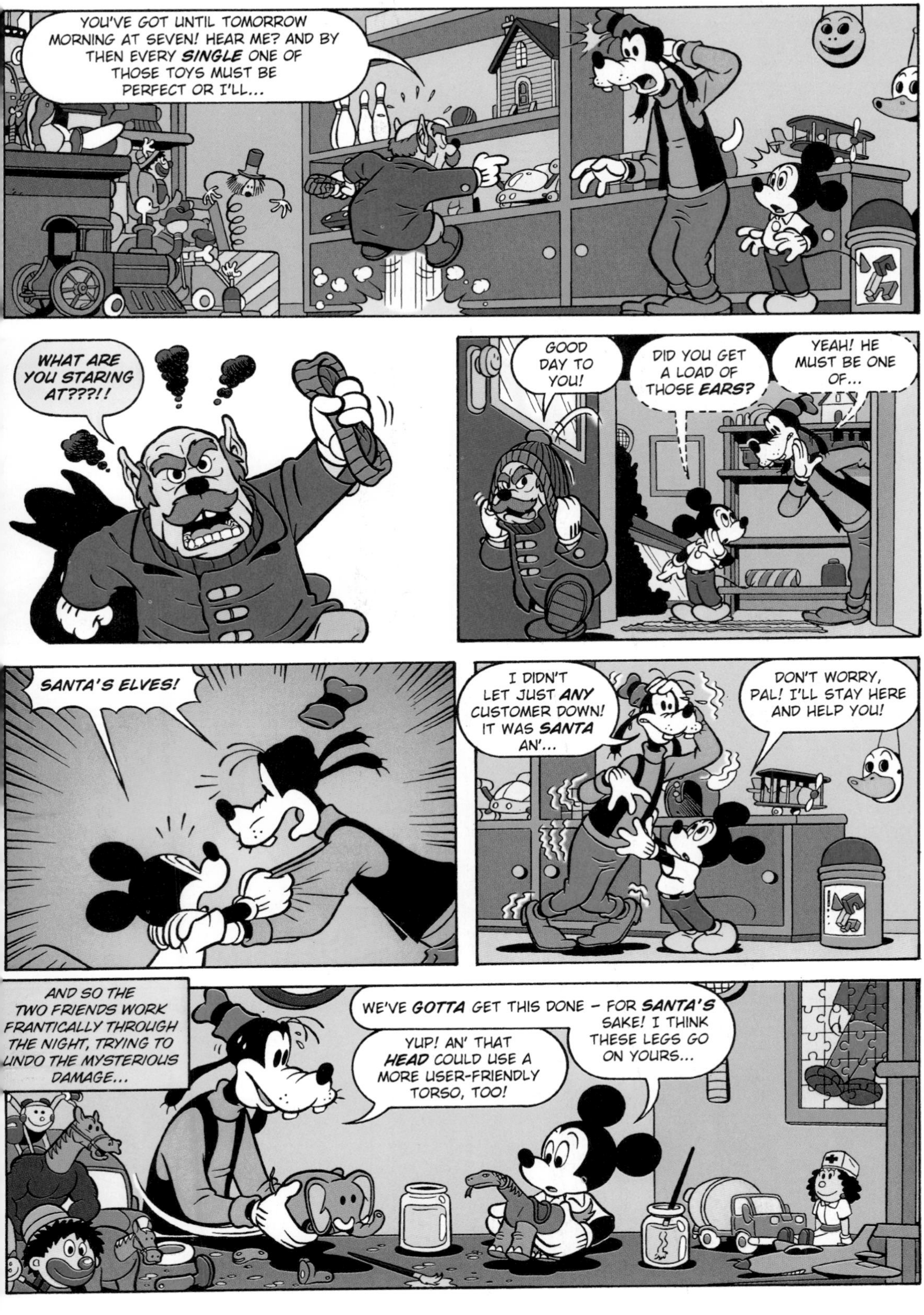
YOU'VE GOT UNTIL TOMORROW MORNING AT SEVEN! HEAR ME? AND BY THEN EVERY SINGLE ONE OF THOSE TOYS MUST BE PERFECT OR I'LL...
WHAT ARE YOU STARING AT???!!
GOOD DAY TO YOU!
DID YOU GET A LOAD OF THOSE EARS?
YEAH! HE MUST BE ONE OF...
SANTA'S ELVES!
I DIDN'T LET JUST ANY CUSTOMER DOWN! IT WAS SANTA AN'...
DON'T WORRY, PAL! I'LL STAY HERE AND HELP YOU!
AND SO THE TWO FRIENDS WORK FRANTICALLY THROUGH THE NIGHT, TRYING TO UNDO THE MYSTERIOUS DAMAGE...
WE'VE GOTTA GET THIS DONE – FOR SANTA'S SAKE! I THINK THESE LEGS GO ON YOURS...
YUP! AN' THAT HEAD COULD USE A MORE USER-FRIENDLY TORSO, TOO!

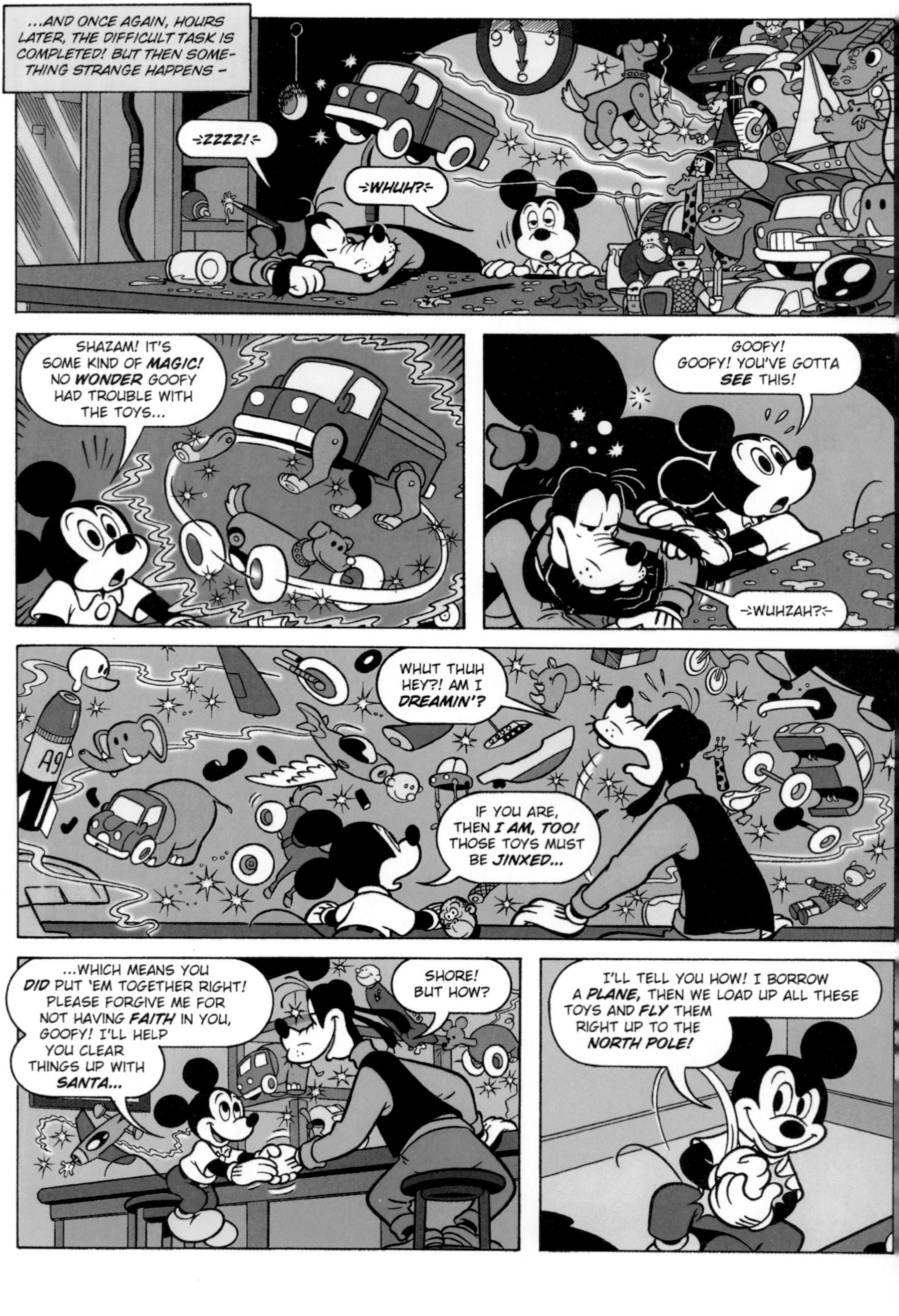

...AND ONCE AGAIN, HOURS LATER, THE DIFFICULT TASK IS COMPLETED! BUT THEN SOME-THING STRANGE HAPPENS –
-ZZZZ!-
-WHUH?-
SHAZAM! IT'S SOME KIND OF MAGIC! NO WONDER GOOFY HAD TROUBLE WITH THE TOYS...
GOOFY! GOOFY! YOU'VE GOTTA SEE THIS!
-WUHZAH?-
WHUT THUH HEY?! AM I DREAMIN'?
IF YOU ARE, THEN I AM, TOO! THOSE TOYS MUST BE JINXED...
...WHICH MEANS YOU DID PUT 'EM TOGETHER RIGHT! PLEASE FORGIVE ME FOR NOT HAVING FAITH IN YOU, GOOFY! I'LL HELP YOU CLEAR THINGS UP WITH SANTA...
SHORE! BUT HOW?
I'LL TELL YOU HOW! I BORROW A PLANE, THEN WE LOAD UP ALL THESE TOYS AND FLY THEM RIGHT UP TO THE NORTH POLE!

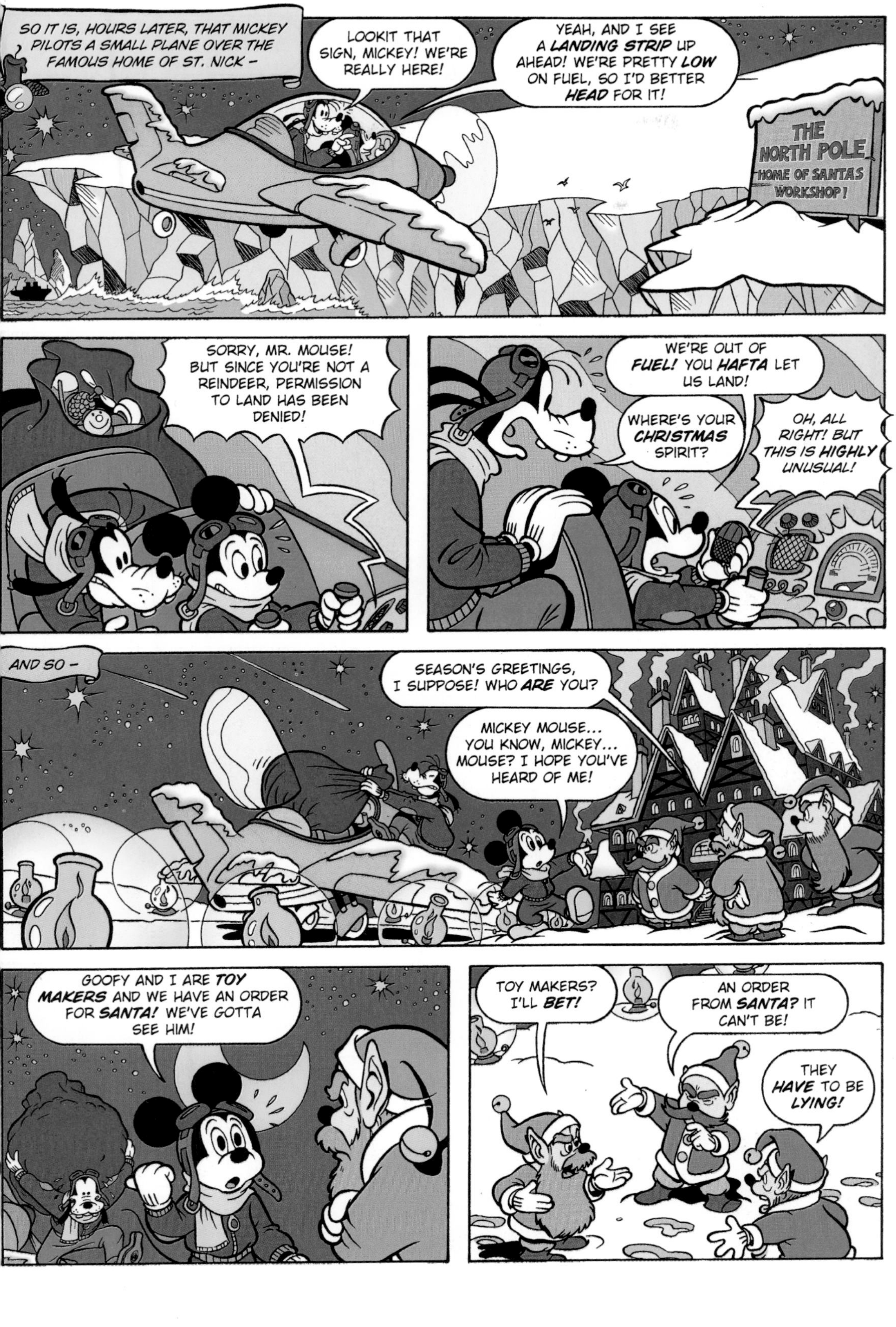
SO IT IS, HOURS LATER, THAT MICKEY PILOTS A SMALL PLANE OVER THE FAMOUS HOME OF ST. NICK –
LOOKIT THAT SIGN, MICKEY! WE'RE REALLY HERE!
YEAH, AND I SEE A LANDING STRIP UP AHEAD! WE'RE PRETTY LOW ON FUEL, SO I'D BETTER HEAD FOR IT!
THE NORTH POLE HOME OF SANTAS WORKSHOP!
SORRY, MR. MOUSE! BUT SINCE YOU'RE NOT A REINDEER, PERMISSION TO LAND HAS BEEN DENIED!
WE'RE OUT OF FUEL! YOU HAFTA LET US LAND!
WHERE'S YOUR CHRISTMAS SPIRIT?
OH, ALL RIGHT! BUT THIS IS HIGHLY UNUSUAL!
AND SO –
SEASON'S GREETINGS, I SUPPOSE! WHO ARE YOU?
MICKEY MOUSE... YOU KNOW, MICKEY... MOUSE? I HOPE YOU'VE HEARD OF ME!
GOOFY AND I ARE TOY MAKERS AND WE HAVE AN ORDER FOR SANTA! WE'VE GOTTA SEE HIM!
TOY MAKERS? I'LL BET!
AN ORDER FROM SANTA? IT CAN'T BE!
THEY HAVE TO BE LYING!

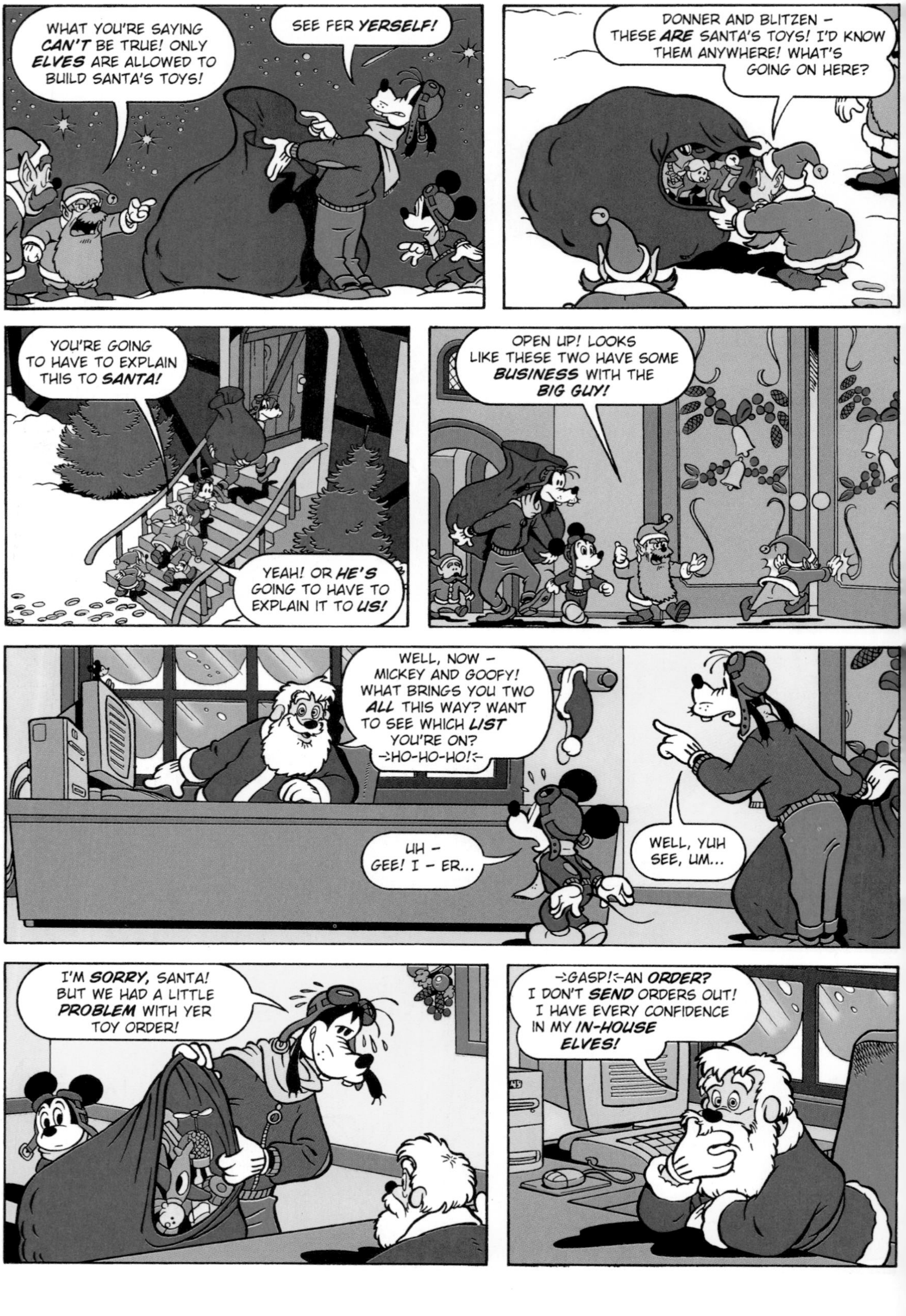
WHAT YOU'RE SAYING CAN'T BE TRUE! ONLY ELVES ARE ALLOWED TO BUILD SANTA'S TOYS!
SEE FER YERSELF!
DONNER AND BLITZEN – THESE ARE SANTA'S TOYS! I'D KNOW THEM ANYWHERE! WHAT'S GOING ON HERE?
YOU'RE GOING TO HAVE TO EXPLAIN THIS TO SANTA!
YEAH! OR HE'S GOING TO HAVE TO EXPLAIN IT TO US!
OPEN UP! LOOKS LIKE THESE TWO HAVE SOME BUSINESS WITH THE BIG GUY!
WELL, NOW – MICKEY AND GOOFY! WHAT BRINGS YOU TWO ALL THIS WAY? WANT TO SEE WHICH LIST YOU'RE ON? -HO-HO-HO!-
UH – GEE! I – ER...
WELL, YUH SEE, UM...
I'M SORRY, SANTA! BUT WE HAD A LITTLE PROBLEM WITH YER TOY ORDER!
-GASP!- AN ORDER? I DON'T SEND ORDERS OUT! I HAVE EVERY CONFIDENCE IN MY IN-HOUSE ELVES!

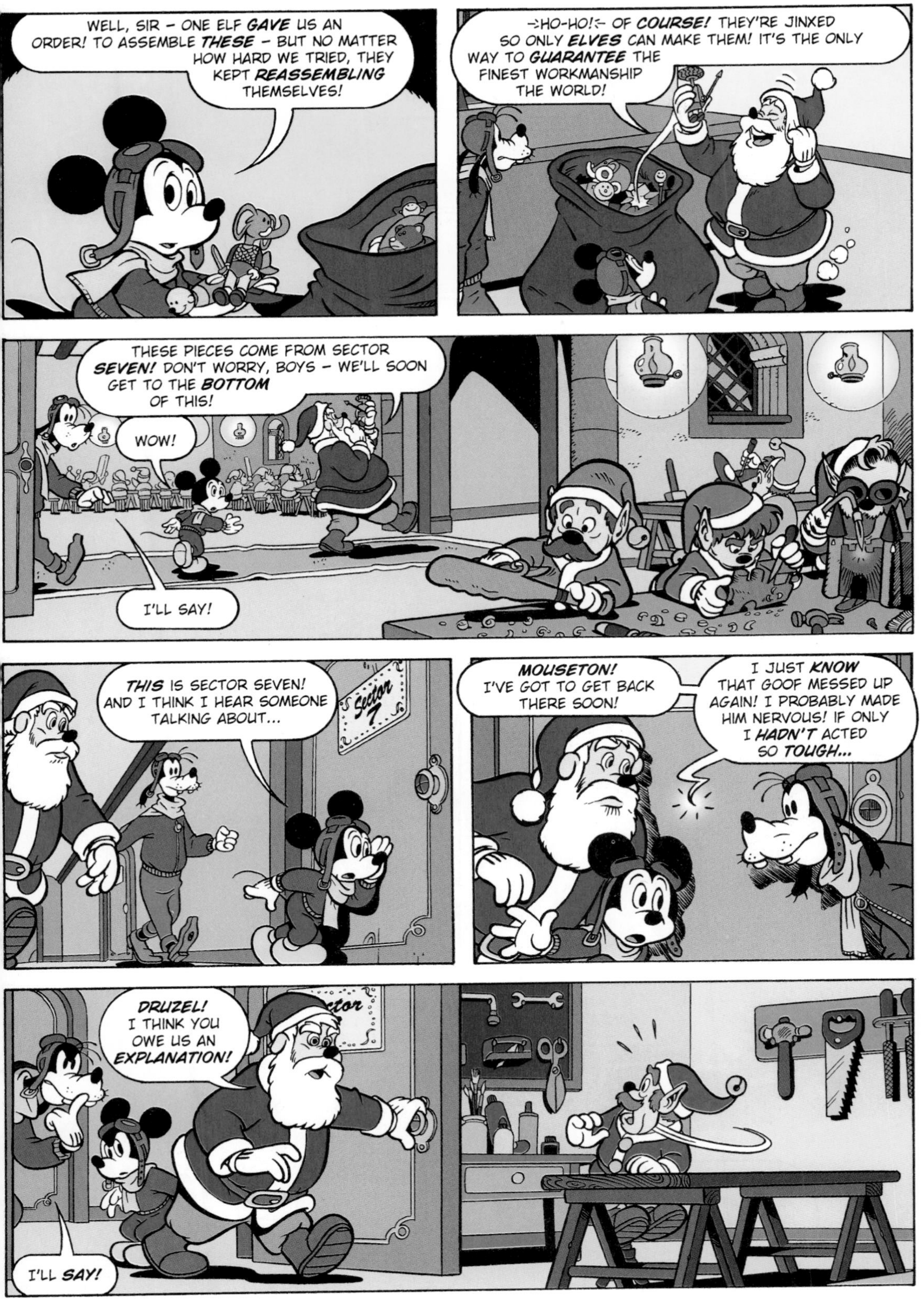

WELL, SIR – ONE ELF GAVE US AN ORDER! TO ASSEMBLE THESE – BUT NO MATTER HOW HARD WE TRIED, THEY KEPT REASSEMBLING THEMSELVES!
-HO-HO!- OF COURSE! THEY'RE JINXED SO ONLY ELVES CAN MAKE THEM! IT'S THE ONLY WAY TO GUARANTEE THE FINEST WORKMANSHIP THE WORLD!
THESE PIECES COME FROM SECTOR SEVEN! DON'T WORRY, BOYS – WE'LL SOON GET TO THE BOTTOM OF THIS!
WOW!
I'LL SAY!
THIS IS SECTOR SEVEN! AND I THINK I HEAR SOMEONE TALKING ABOUT...
Sector 7
MOUSETON! I'VE GOT TO GET BACK THERE SOON!
I JUST KNOW THAT GOOF MESSED UP AGAIN! I PROBABLY MADE HIM NERVOUS! IF ONLY I HADN'T ACTED SO TOUGH...
DRUZEL! I THINK YOU OWE US AN EXPLANATION!
I'LL SAY!

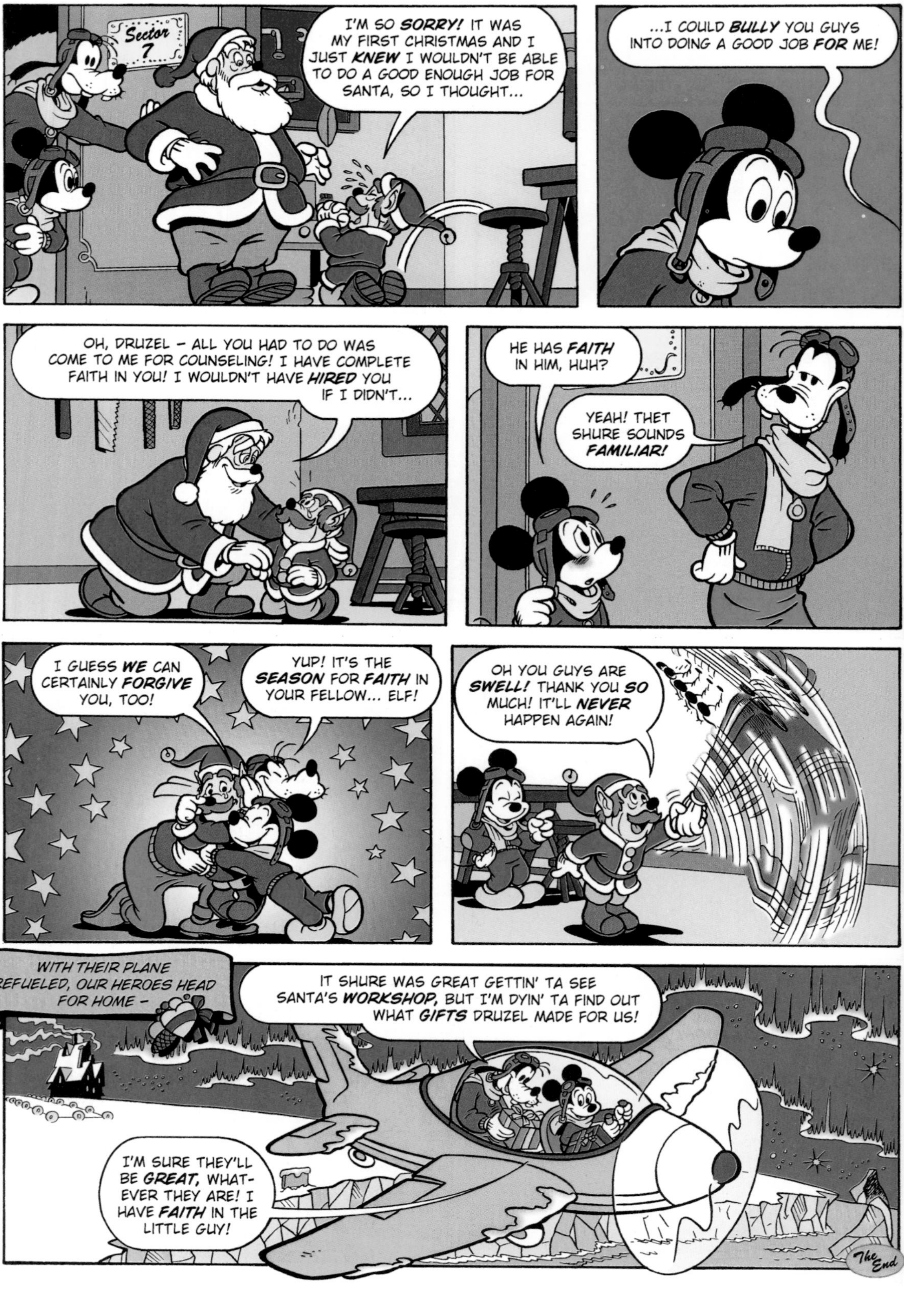
I'M SO SORRY! IT WAS MY FIRST CHRISTMAS AND I JUST KNEW I WOULDN'T BE ABLE TO DO A GOOD ENOUGH JOB FOR SANTA, SO I THOUGHT...
Sector 7
...I COULD BULLY YOU GUYS INTO DOING A GOOD JOB FOR ME!
OH, DRUZEL – ALL YOU HAD TO DO WAS COME TO ME FOR COUNSELING! I HAVE COMPLETE FAITH IN YOU! I WOULDN'T HAVE HIRED YOU IF I DIDN'T...
HE HAS FAITH IN HIM, HUH?
YEAH! THET SHURE SOUNDS FAMILIAR!
I GUESS WE CAN CERTAINLY FORGIVE YOU, TOO!
YUP! IT'S THE SEASON FOR FAITH IN YOUR FELLOW... ELF!
OH YOU GUYS ARE SWELL! THANK YOU SO MUCH! IT'LL NEVER HAPPEN AGAIN!
WITH THEIR PLANE REFUELED, OUR HEROES HEAD FOR HOME –
IT SHURE WAS GREAT GETTIN' TA SEE SANTA'S WORKSHOP, BUT I'M DYIN' TA FIND OUT WHAT GIFTS DRUZEL MADE FOR US!
I'M SURE THEY'LL BE GREAT, WHAT-EVER THEY ARE! I HAVE FAITH IN THE LITTLE GUY!
The End

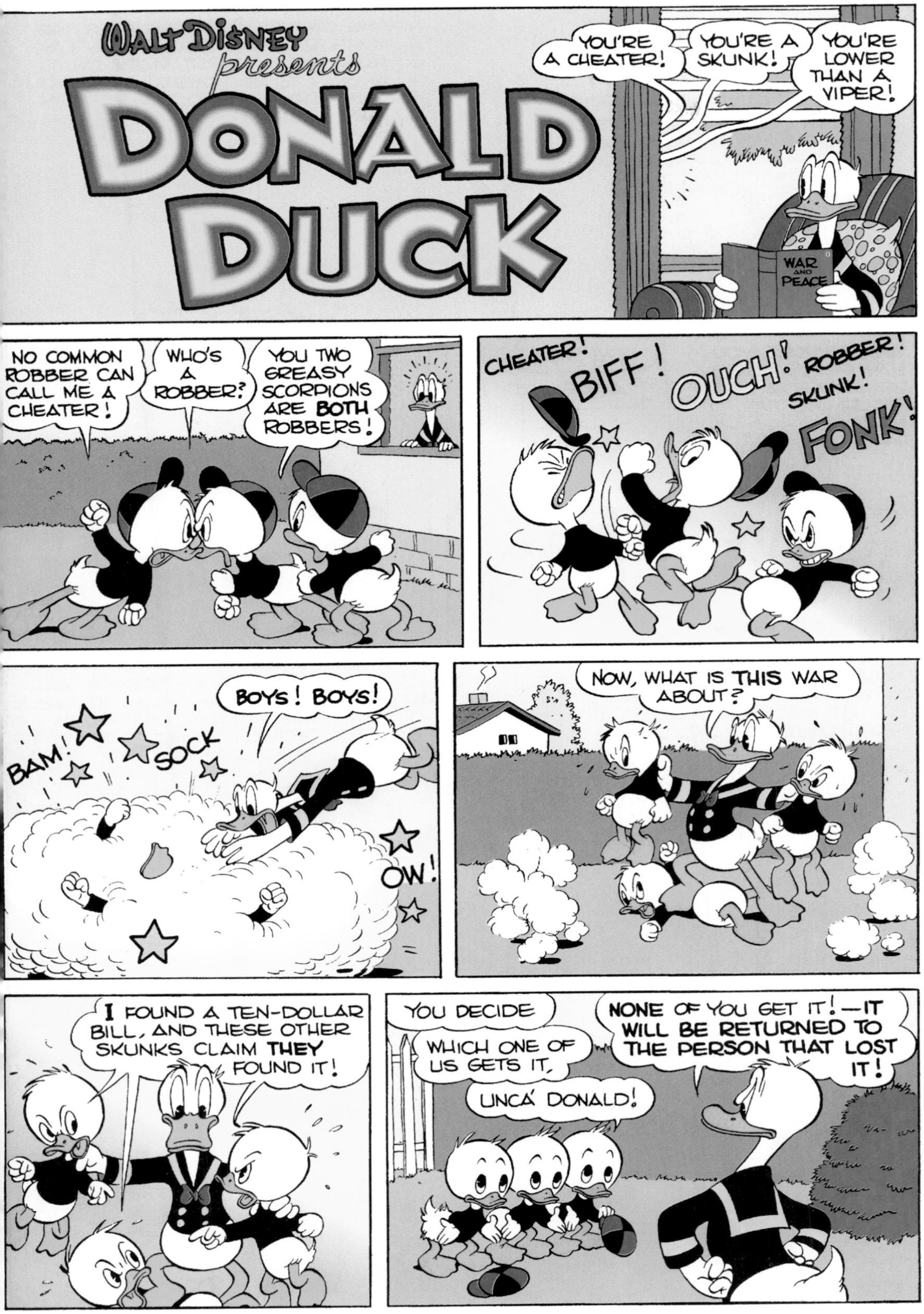
WALT DISNEY presents
DONALD DUCK
YOU'RE A CHEATER!
YOU'RE A SKUNK!
YOU'RE LOWER THAN A VIPER!
WAR AND PEACE
NO COMMON ROBBER CAN CALL ME A CHEATER!
WHO'S A ROBBER?
YOU TWO GREASY SCORPIONS ARE BOTH ROBBERS!
CHEATER!
BIFF!
OUCH!
ROBBER!
SKUNK!
FONK!
BAM!
SOCK
BOYS! BOYS!
OW!
NOW, WHAT IS THIS WAR ABOUT?
I FOUND A TEN-DOLLAR BILL, AND THESE OTHER SKUNKS CLAIM THEY FOUND IT!
YOU DECIDE
WHICH ONE OF US GETS IT,
UNCA' DONALD!
NONE OF YOU GET IT!—IT WILL BE RETURNED TO THE PERSON THAT LOST IT!

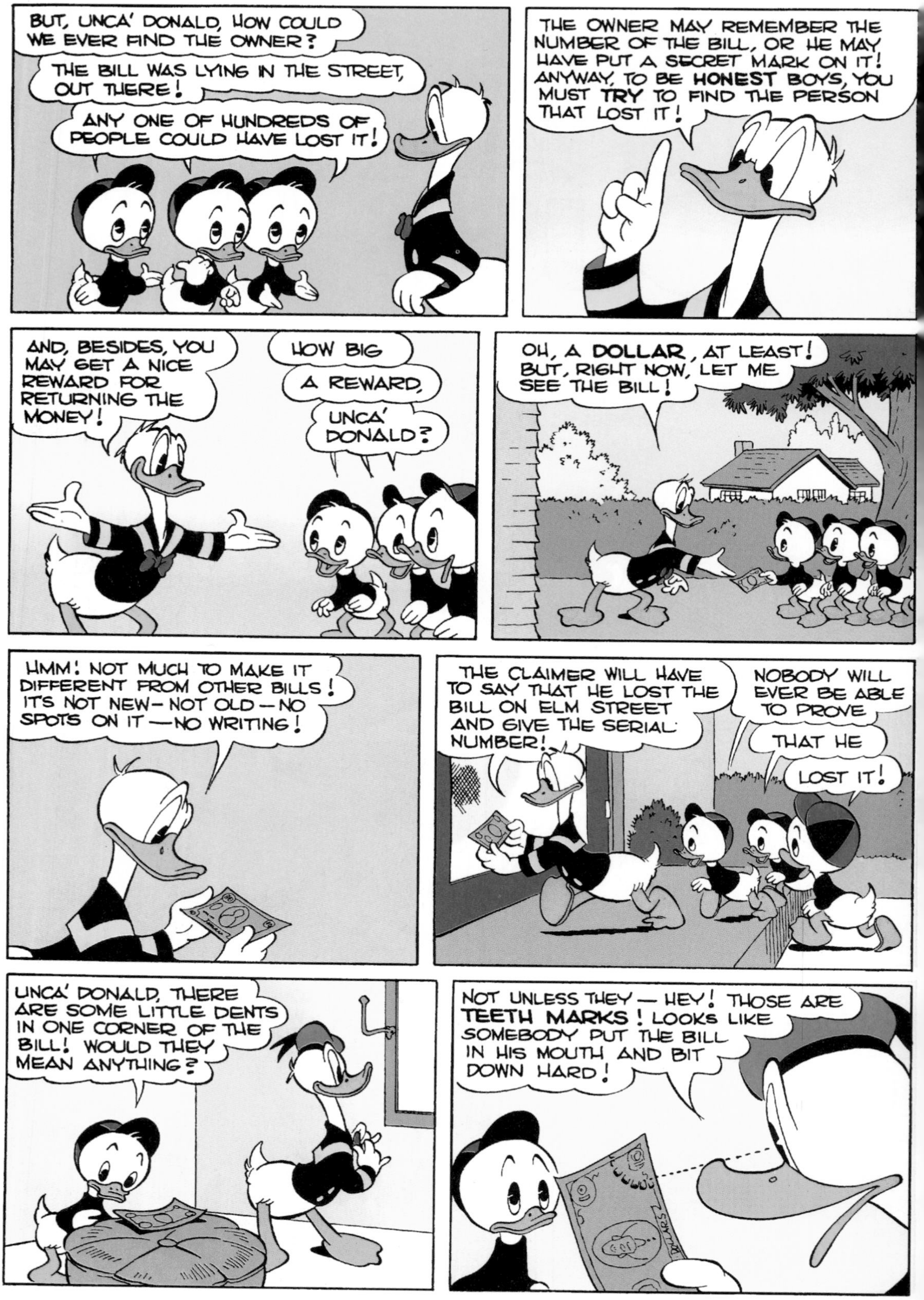
BUT, UNCA' DONALD, HOW COULD WE EVER FIND THE OWNER?
THE BILL WAS LYING IN THE STREET, OUT THERE!
ANY ONE OF HUNDREDS OF PEOPLE COULD HAVE LOST IT!
THE OWNER MAY REMEMBER THE NUMBER OF THE BILL, OR HE MAY HAVE PUT A SECRET MARK ON IT! ANYWAY, TO BE HONEST BOYS, YOU MUST TRY TO FIND THE PERSON THAT LOST IT!
AND, BESIDES, YOU MAY GET A NICE REWARD FOR RETURNING THE MONEY!
HOW BIG
A REWARD,
UNCA' DONALD?
OH, A DOLLAR, AT LEAST! BUT, RIGHT NOW, LET ME SEE THE BILL!
HMM! NOT MUCH TO MAKE IT DIFFERENT FROM OTHER BILLS! ITS NOT NEW—NOT OLD—NO SPOTS ON IT—NO WRITING!
THE CLAIMER WILL HAVE TO SAY THAT HE LOST THE BILL ON ELM STREET AND GIVE THE SERIAL NUMBER!
NOBODY WILL EVER BE ABLE TO PROVE
THAT HE
LOST IT!
UNCA' DONALD, THERE ARE SOME LITTLE DENTS IN ONE CORNER OF THE BILL! WOULD THEY MEAN ANYTHING?
NOT UNLESS THEY — HEY! THOSE ARE TEETH MARKS! LOOKS LIKE SOMEBODY PUT THE BILL IN HIS MOUTH AND BIT DOWN HARD!

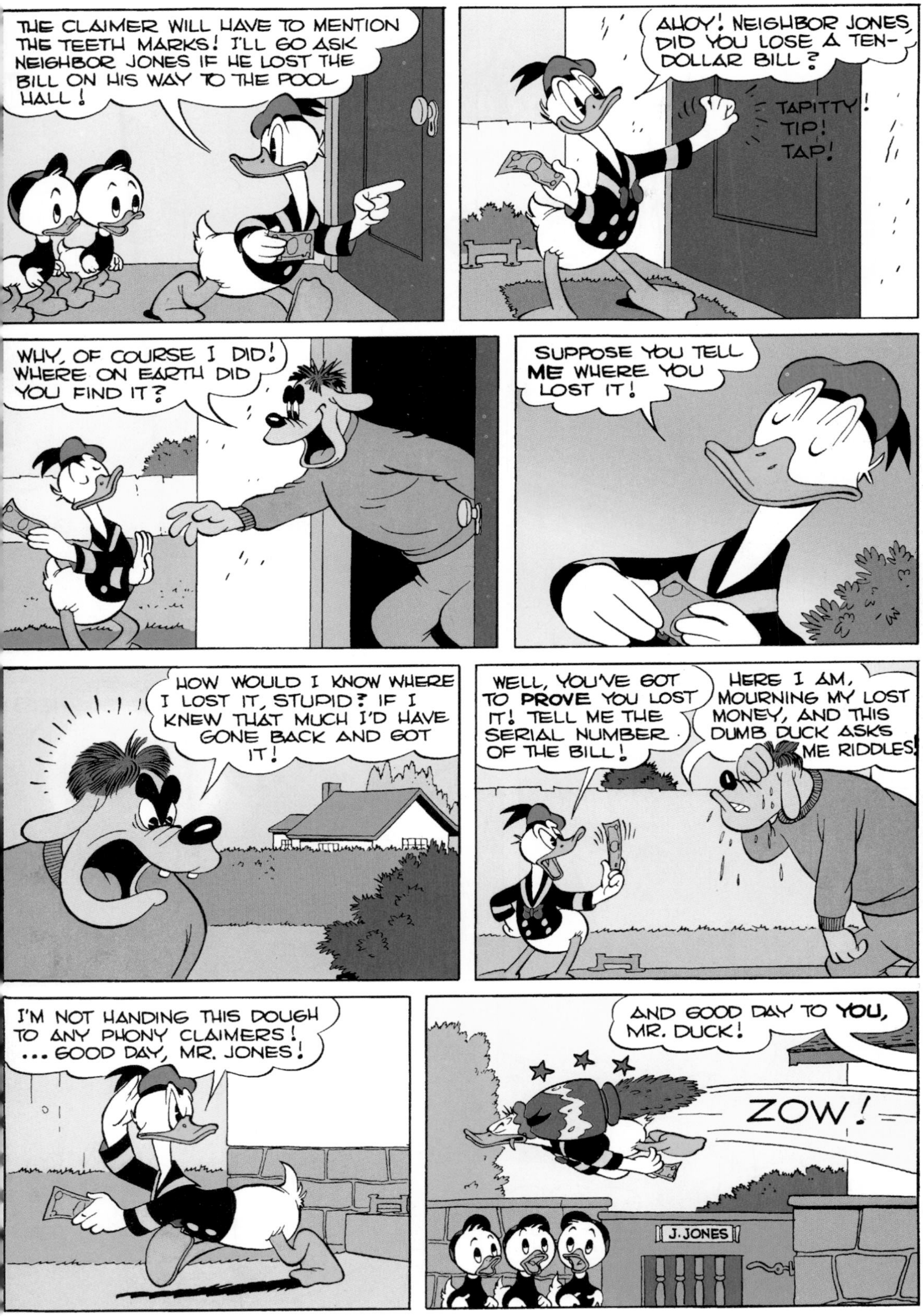
THE CLAIMER WILL HAVE TO MENTION THE TEETH MARKS! I'LL GO ASK NEIGHBOR JONES IF HE LOST THE BILL ON HIS WAY TO THE POOL HALL!
AHOY! NEIGHBOR JONES, DID YOU LOSE A TEN-DOLLAR BILL?
TAPITTY! TIP! TAP!
WHY, OF COURSE I DID! WHERE ON EARTH DID YOU FIND IT?
SUPPOSE YOU TELL ME WHERE YOU LOST IT!
HOW WOULD I KNOW WHERE I LOST IT, STUPID? IF I KNEW THAT MUCH I'D HAVE GONE BACK AND GOT IT!
WELL, YOU'VE GOT TO PROVE YOU LOST IT! TELL ME THE SERIAL NUMBER OF THE BILL!
HERE I AM, MOURNING MY LOST MONEY, AND THIS DUMB DUCK ASKS ME RIDDLES!
I'M NOT HANDING THIS DOUGH TO ANY PHONY CLAIMERS! ... GOOD DAY, MR. JONES!
AND GOOD DAY TO YOU, MR. DUCK!
ZOW!
J. JONES

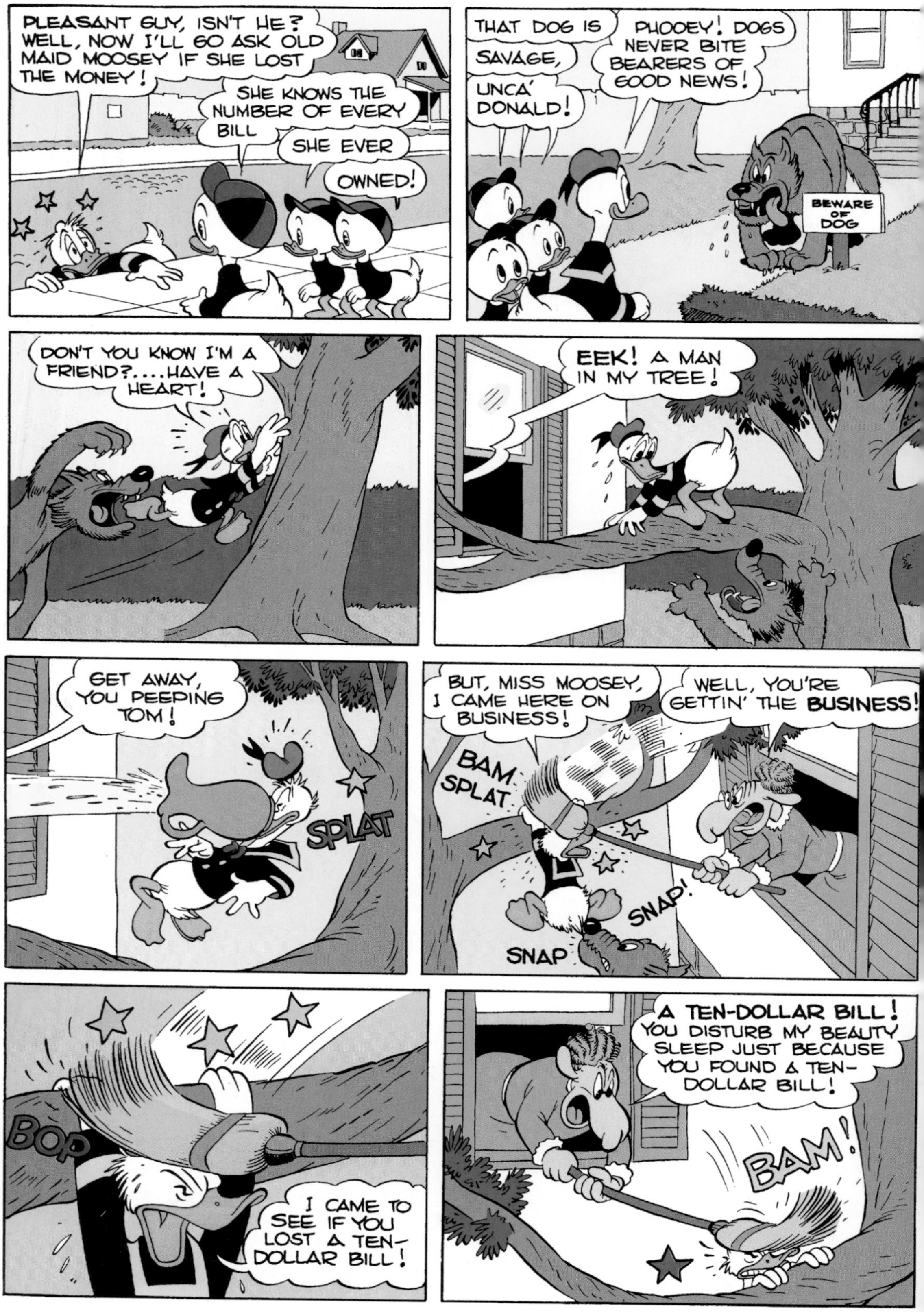
PLEASANT GUY, ISN'T HE? WELL, NOW I'LL GO ASK OLD MAID MOOSEY IF SHE LOST THE MONEY!
SHE KNOWS THE NUMBER OF EVERY BILL
SHE EVER
OWNED!
THAT DOG IS SAVAGE,
UNCA' DONALD!
PHOOEY! DOGS NEVER BITE BEARERS OF GOOD NEWS!
BEWARE OF DOG
DON'T YOU KNOW I'M A FRIEND?....HAVE A HEART!
EEK! A MAN IN MY TREE!
GET AWAY, YOU PEEPING TOM!
SPLAT
BUT, MISS MOOSEY, I CAME HERE ON BUSINESS!
WELL, YOU'RE GETTIN' THE **BUSINESS**!
BAM
SPLAT
SNAP!
SNAP
BOP
I CAME TO SEE IF YOU LOST A TEN-DOLLAR BILL!
A TEN-DOLLAR BILL! YOU DISTURB MY BEAUTY SLEEP JUST BECAUSE YOU FOUND A TEN-DOLLAR BILL!
BAM!

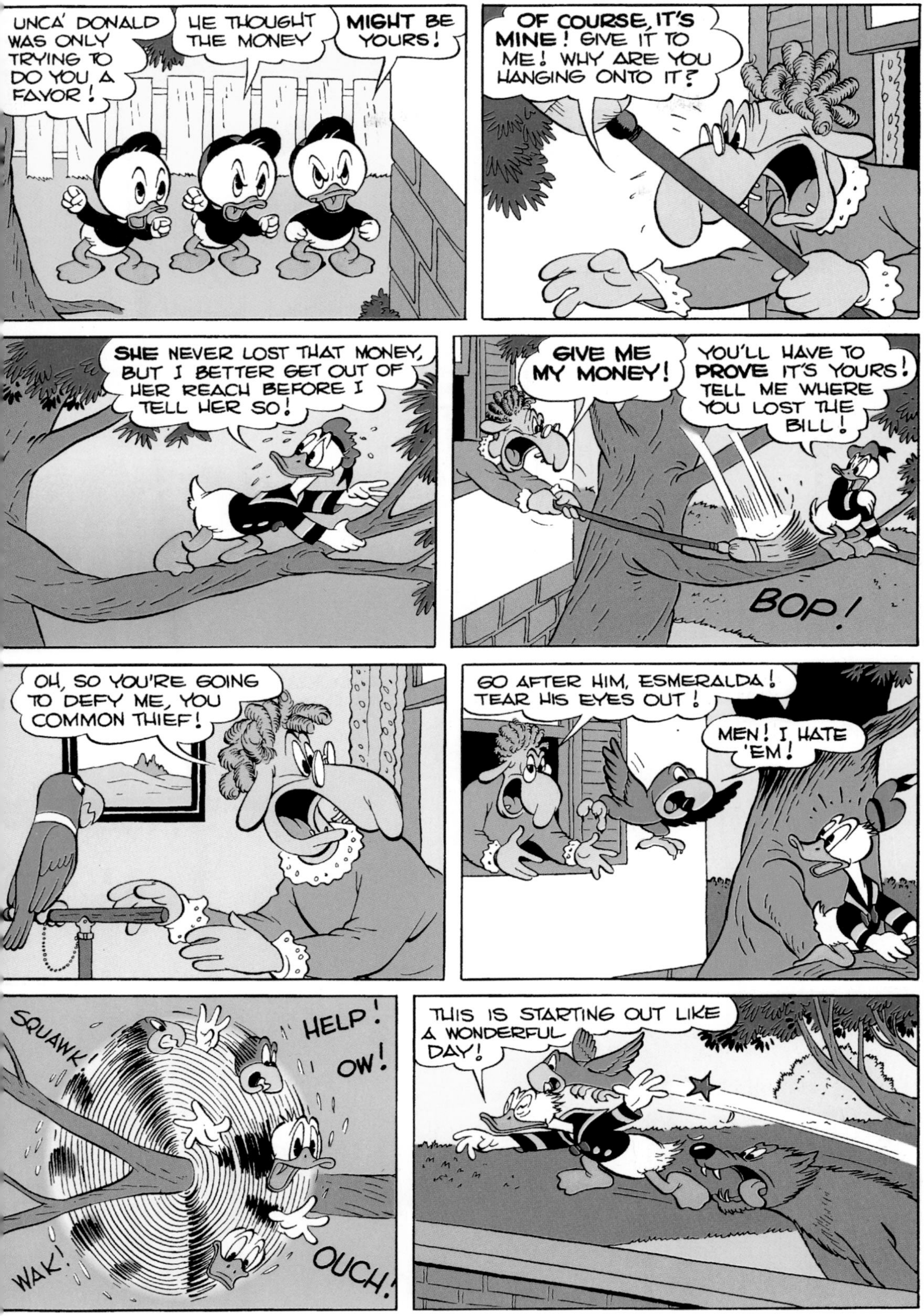
UNCA' DONALD WAS ONLY TRYING TO DO YOU A FAVOR!
HE THOUGHT THE MONEY
MIGHT BE YOURS!
OF COURSE, IT'S MINE! GIVE IT TO ME! WHY ARE YOU HANGING ONTO IT?
SHE NEVER LOST THAT MONEY, BUT I BETTER GET OUT OF HER REACH BEFORE I TELL HER SO!
GIVE ME MY MONEY!
YOU'LL HAVE TO PROVE IT'S YOURS! TELL ME WHERE YOU LOST THE BILL!
BOP!
OH, SO YOU'RE GOING TO DEFY ME, YOU COMMON THIEF!
GO AFTER HIM, ESMERALDA! TEAR HIS EYES OUT!
MEN! I HATE 'EM!
SQUAWK!
HELP!
OW!
WAK!
OUCH!
THIS IS STARTING OUT LIKE A WONDERFUL DAY!

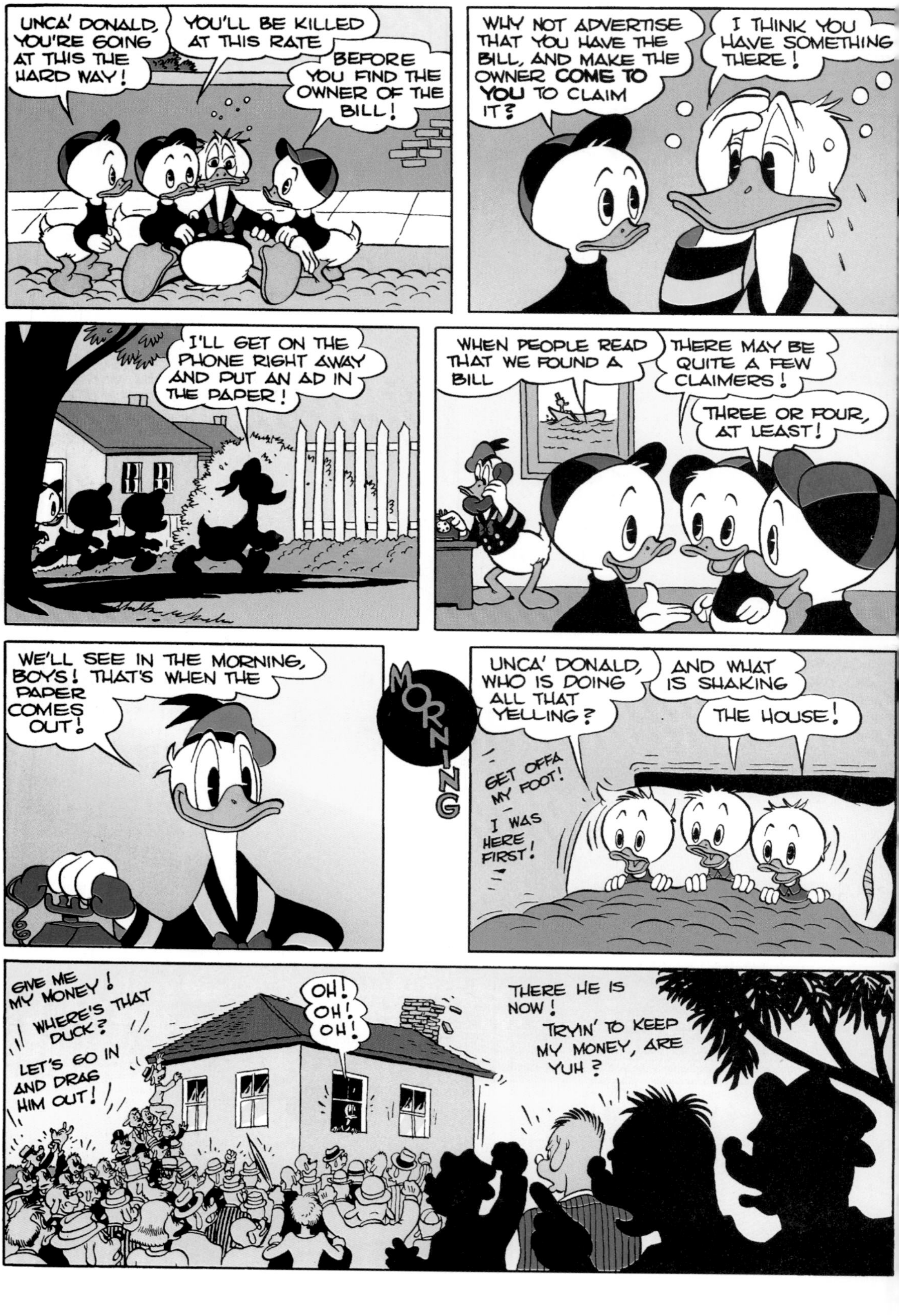
UNCA' DONALD, YOU'RE GOING AT THIS THE HARD WAY!
YOU'LL BE KILLED AT THIS RATE
BEFORE YOU FIND THE OWNER OF THE BILL!
WHY NOT ADVERTISE THAT YOU HAVE THE BILL, AND MAKE THE OWNER COME TO YOU TO CLAIM IT?
I THINK YOU HAVE SOMETHING THERE!
I'LL GET ON THE PHONE RIGHT AWAY AND PUT AN AD IN THE PAPER!
WHEN PEOPLE READ THAT WE FOUND A BILL
THERE MAY BE QUITE A FEW CLAIMERS!
THREE OR FOUR, AT LEAST!
WE'LL SEE IN THE MORNING, BOYS! THAT'S WHEN THE PAPER COMES OUT!
MORNING
UNCA' DONALD, WHO IS DOING ALL THAT YELLING?
AND WHAT IS SHAKING
THE HOUSE!
GET OFFA MY FOOT!
I WAS HERE FIRST!
GIVE ME MY MONEY!
WHERE'S THAT DUCK?
LET'S GO IN AND DRAG HIM OUT!
OH! OH! OH!
THERE HE IS NOW!
TRYIN' TO KEEP MY MONEY, ARE YUH?

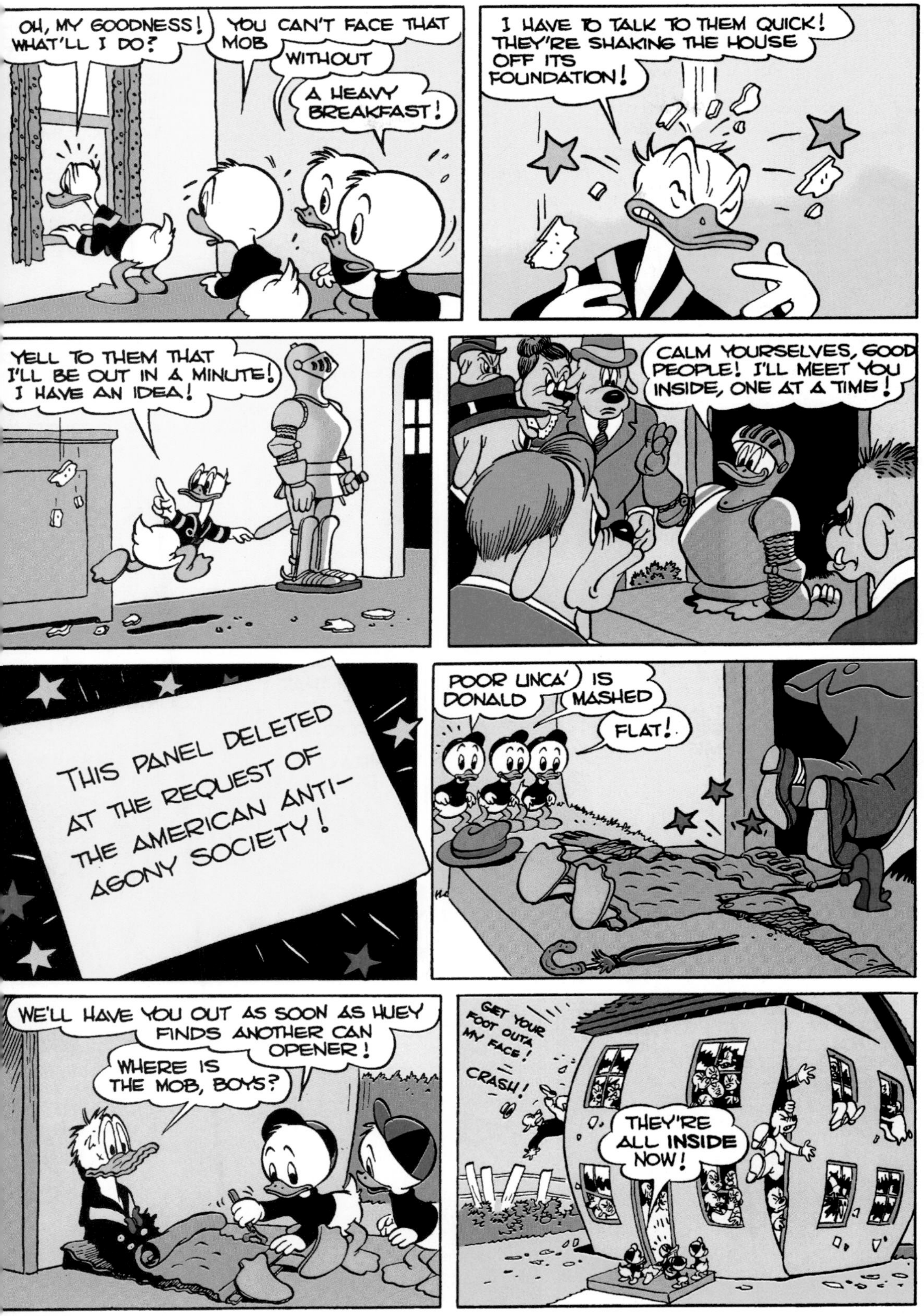
OH, MY GOODNESS! WHAT'LL I DO?
YOU CAN'T FACE THAT MOB
WITHOUT
A HEAVY BREAKFAST!
I HAVE TO TALK TO THEM QUICK! THEY'RE SHAKING THE HOUSE OFF ITS FOUNDATION!
YELL TO THEM THAT I'LL BE OUT IN A MINUTE! I HAVE AN IDEA!
CALM YOURSELVES, GOOD PEOPLE! I'LL MEET YOU INSIDE, ONE AT A TIME!
THIS PANEL DELETED AT THE REQUEST OF THE AMERICAN ANTI-AGONY SOCIETY!
POOR UNCA' DONALD
IS MASHED
FLAT!
WE'LL HAVE YOU OUT AS SOON AS HUEY FINDS ANOTHER CAN OPENER!
WHERE IS THE MOB, BOYS?
GET YOUR FOOT OUTA MY FACE!
CRASH!
THEY'RE ALL INSIDE NOW!

WHY NOT HAVE THESE PEOPLE DRAW NUMBERS

AND LINE UP ACCORDINGLY?

WISE WORDS FROM THE MOUTHS OF BABES!

THE MOB COMPLIES, BUT AFTER HOURS OF GRILLING NOBODY HAS PROVED HIS CLAIM TO THE BILL!

WHY NOT GIVE UP AND KEEP THE BILL, UNCA' DONALD?

YOU'LL NEVER FIND THE TRUE OWNER!

I'LL KEEP TRYING, ALTHOUGH I'M GETTING MAD AT ALL THESE PHONY CLAIMERS.

SOMEDAY SOMEONE WILL COME ALONG AND SAY: "I LOST A BILL ON ELM STREET! IT WAS NUMBER K2367948 B AND HAD A SET OF TEETH MARKS IN ONE CORNER!"

HELLO! I CAME IN TO SEE IF YOU FOUND DE BILL I LOST ON ELM STREET! IT WAS NUMBER K2367948 B AND HAD A SET OF TEETH MARKS IN ONE CORNER!

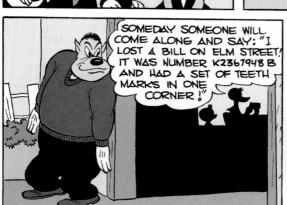

IT GIVES ME GREAT PLEASURE TO RETURN THIS BILL TO ITS PROPER OWNER!

T'ANKS! HERE'S A DIME FER YER TROUBLE!

ALL OF THAT GRIEF

FOR A MEASLY DIME!

AND I THINK IT'S A COUNTERFEIT! LOOK AT IT BEND!

HEH! HEH!

NOBODY WHO IS THAT CHEAP COULD BE HONEST! I'M GOIN' TO FOLLOW THAT GUY AND SEE WHAT I CAN SEE!

HE IS MEETING ANOTHER GUY! I'LL LISTEN TO WHAT THEY SAY!

DID YOU SWINDLE DE TEN FROM DAT DUMB DUCK, BUTCH?

SURE DID! NOW WE KIN BUY A GUN AN' ROB DE ORPHINTS' HOME!

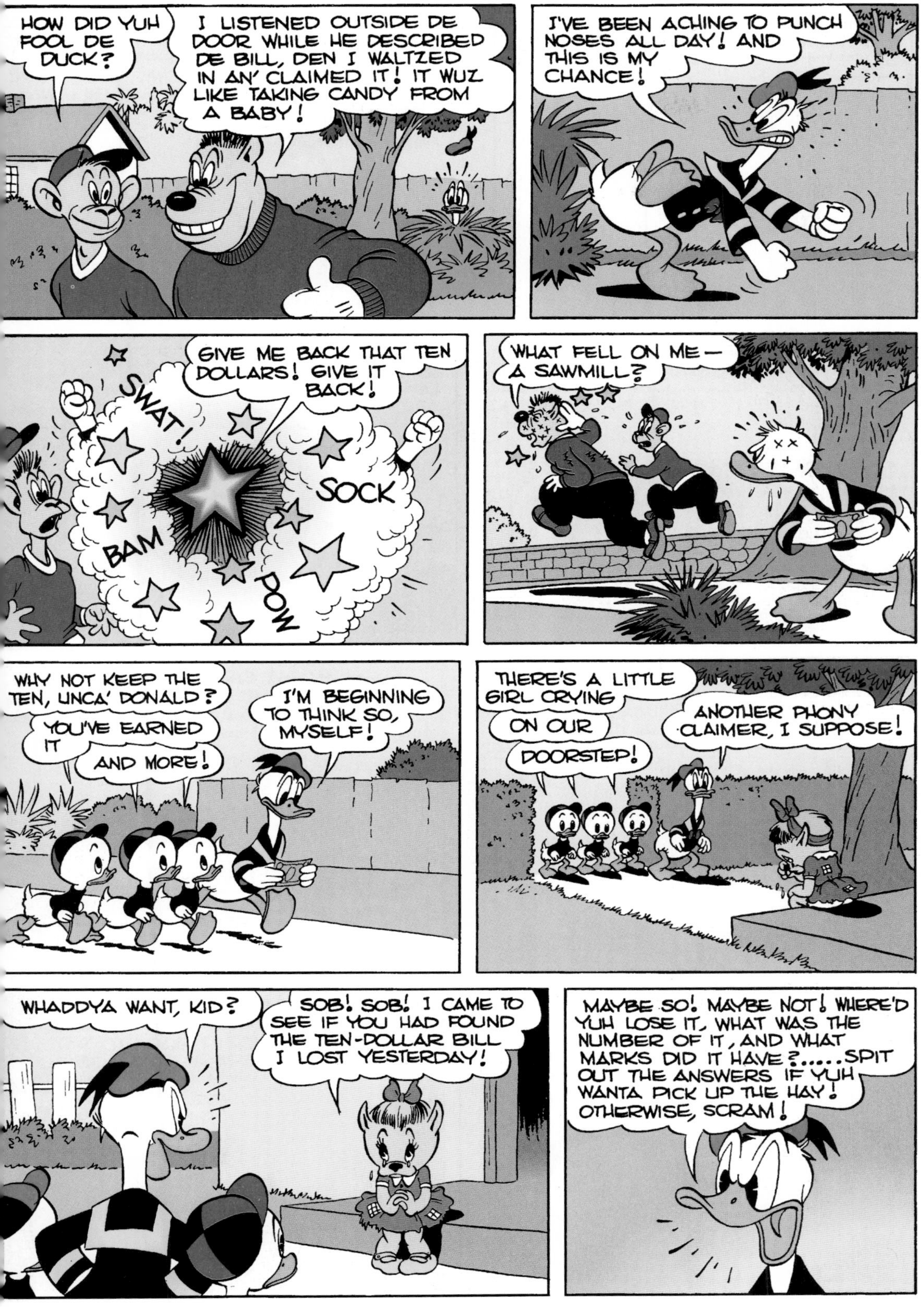
HOW DID YUH FOOL DE DUCK?
I LISTENED OUTSIDE DE DOOR WHILE HE DESCRIBED DE BILL, DEN I WALTZED IN AN' CLAIMED IT! IT WUZ LIKE TAKING CANDY FROM A BABY!
I'VE BEEN ACHING TO PUNCH NOSES ALL DAY! AND THIS IS MY CHANCE!
GIVE ME BACK THAT TEN DOLLARS! GIVE IT BACK!
SWAT!
SOCK
BAM
POW
WHAT FELL ON ME— A SAWMILL?
WHY NOT KEEP THE TEN, UNCA' DONALD?
YOU'VE EARNED IT
AND MORE!
I'M BEGINNING TO THINK SO, MYSELF!
THERE'S A LITTLE GIRL CRYING
ON OUR
DOORSTEP!
ANOTHER PHONY CLAIMER, I SUPPOSE!
WHADDYA WANT, KID?
SOB! SOB! I CAME TO SEE IF YOU HAD FOUND THE TEN-DOLLAR BILL I LOST YESTERDAY!
MAYBE SO! MAYBE NOT! WHERE'D YUH LOSE IT, WHAT WAS THE NUMBER OF IT, AND WHAT MARKS DID IT HAVE?.....SPIT OUT THE ANSWERS IF YUH WANTA PICK UP THE HAY! OTHERWISE, SCRAM!

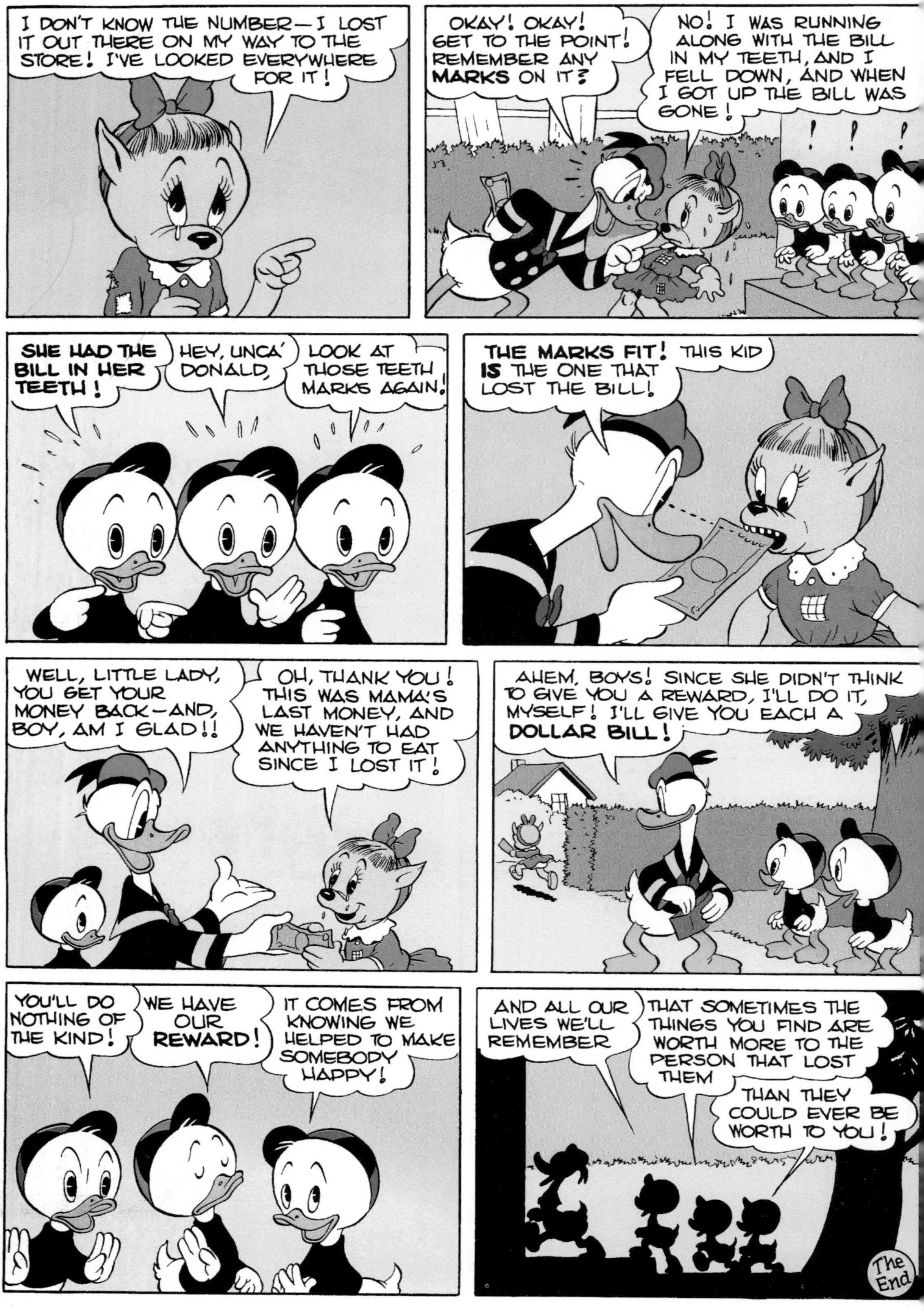
I DON'T KNOW THE NUMBER—I LOST IT OUT THERE ON MY WAY TO THE STORE! I'VE LOOKED EVERYWHERE FOR IT!
OKAY! OKAY! GET TO THE POINT! REMEMBER ANY **MARKS** ON IT?
NO! I WAS RUNNING ALONG WITH THE BILL IN MY TEETH, AND I FELL DOWN, AND WHEN I GOT UP THE BILL WAS GONE!
! ! !
SHE HAD THE BILL IN HER TEETH!
HEY, UNCA' DONALD,
LOOK AT THOSE TEETH MARKS AGAIN!
THE MARKS FIT! THIS KID **IS** THE ONE THAT LOST THE BILL!
WELL, LITTLE LADY, YOU GET YOUR MONEY BACK—AND, BOY, AM I GLAD!!
OH, THANK YOU! THIS WAS MAMA'S LAST MONEY, AND WE HAVEN'T HAD ANYTHING TO EAT SINCE I LOST IT!
AHEM, BOYS! SINCE SHE DIDN'T THINK TO GIVE YOU A REWARD, I'LL DO IT, MYSELF! I'LL GIVE YOU EACH A **DOLLAR BILL**!
YOU'LL DO NOTHING OF THE KIND!
WE HAVE OUR **REWARD**!
IT COMES FROM KNOWING WE HELPED TO MAKE SOMEBODY HAPPY!
AND ALL OUR LIVES WE'LL REMEMBER
THAT SOMETIMES THE THINGS YOU FIND ARE WORTH MORE TO THE PERSON THAT LOST THEM
THAN THEY COULD EVER BE WORTH TO YOU!
The End